THE WEBSTER-HAYNE DE[BATE]

WITNESS TO HISTORY

Peter Charles Hoffer and Williamjames Hull Hoffer, *Series Editors*

The

WEBSTER-HAYNE DEBATE

DEFINING NATIONHOOD
IN THE EARLY AMERICAN REPUBLIC

CHRISTOPHER CHILDERS
Pittsburgh State University
Pittsburgh, Kansas

Johns Hopkins University Press | *Baltimore*

© 2018 Johns Hopkins University Press
All rights reserved. Published 2018
Printed in the United States of America on acid-free paper
9 8 7 6 5 4 3 2 1

Johns Hopkins University Press
2715 North Charles Street
Baltimore, Maryland 21218-4363
www.press.jhu.edu

Library of Congress Cataloging-in-Publication data is available.

ISBN-13: 978-1-4214-2613-6 (hc)
ISBN-10: 1-4214-2613-7 (hc)
ISBN-13: 978-1-4214-2614-3 (pb)
ISBN-10: 1-4214-2614-5 (pb)
ISBN-13: 978-1-4214-2615-0 (electronic)
ISBN-10: 1-4214-2615-3 (electronic)

A catalog record for this book is available from the British Library.

Special discounts are available for bulk purchases of this book. For more information, please contact Special Sales at 410-516-6936 or specialsales@press.jhu.edu.

Johns Hopkins University Press uses environmentally friendly book materials, including recycled text paper that is composed of at least 30 percent post-consumer waste, whenever possible.

To Leah, Elyse, Bridget, and Jennifer

CONTENTS

PREFACE

FOR GENERATIONS, SCHOOL CHILDREN memorized passages from Daniel Webster's Second Reply to Robert Y. Hayne because of its soaring articulation of nationalism and American nationhood. Webster, so the story goes, issued a spirited defense of nationalism against the South Carolinian Hayne, his colleague John C. Calhoun, and the nullifiers who sought to dismember the Union for their own sectional interests. Alas, then and now, Webster's dazzling oratory perhaps obscures the underlying meanings of the issues behind what we call the Webster-Hayne Debate.

This book illuminates those underlying meanings by placing the debate in the broader context of the early American republic. Historians have certainly recognized the significance of the debate in terms of the nullification movement and the ongoing struggle in the politics of the early republic over states' rights versus nationalism. In recent histories of the early American republic, the debate usually appears as a relatively minor note within a broader narrative. My book takes an alternative view by focusing on the debate itself and using it as a lens through which we can view the issues of nationalism, sectionalism, and the meaning of union to Americans in the early republic.

In order to understand why Webster and Hayne contested the meaning of the Union in 1830, one must go back to the period after the War of 1812, when nationalism and sectionalism became merged with notions of economic development and the extension of slavery, among other themes. The pages that follow take the reader on a tour of the North, South, and West between 1815 and 1830. The political decline of the New England Federalists and the expansion of the commercial economy in the 1820s frame the northeastern mind-set on nationalism. New England may have retreated to states' rights during the War of 1812 to protect its maritime economy, but after the war its citizens moved toward a muscular political and economic nationalism that shaped its future development. The South, on the other hand, had supported the war and its aims. Some of America's most ardent nationalists during and after the war resided in the southern states. By 1820, however, the South began a slow retreat of its own from nationalism to localism as the southern economy became beset by outside pressures and the politics of slavery reared its head with the admission of Missouri to the Union. For a variety of reasons, southerners came to detest the nationalism of John Quincy Adams and instead supported the states' rights program of Andrew Jackson. Meanwhile, the maturing and growing West had its own concerns by the 1820s. An economic depression that coincided with the Missouri crisis threatened the region's economic stability at the very moment that the extension of slavery threatened the perpetuity of the Union. A compromise calmed the discord over slavery and its extension to the West, but fundamental economic and political concerns remained that centered on the issue of public lands and their availability to the surging mass of citizens moving westward.

The issues of the North, South, and West all contributed to the Webster-Hayne Debate and shaped the remarks of its two chief protagonists and a host of other senators who used the moment to debate virtually the entirety of American politics and political history. Through the debate, the relationship between the sections and the interconnectedness of the issues under consideration become clear. Moreover, understanding the political consequences of the debates will add context and perspective to their meaning and to how politicians sought to address the nature of the Union at a time in which its meaning remained contested.

ACKNOWLEDGMENTS

ONE OF THE MOST REWARDING PARTS of being a historian comes from the friendships one makes in the office, the classroom, the archives, and the libraries. At Benedictine College, Richard Crane, as well as George Nicholas, Steve Mirarchi, and James Young listened to me talk about Webster and Hayne over noon lunches filled with good conversation and cheer. At Pittsburg State University, Kirstin Lawson, Kyle Thompson, and John Daley, as well as my other colleagues have supported my work. My department chair, Barbara Bonnekessen, provided crucial time for research and writing as well as financial support.

Students in two seminar classes on the early American republic at Benedictine College and Pittsburg State University provided an engaging atmosphere to talk through many of the ideas in this book and showed that the early American republic is a vibrant field to study.

Two of the greatest friends I have known deserve special mention. Rachel Shelden took time to listen to my ideas and share her thoughts, something she has willingly done since the first time we met at a conference on James Buchanan in 2007 and became fast friends. Adam Pratt read and commented on the manuscript and helped me formulate ideas from the first moment that I conceived of writing about the Webster-Hayne Debate. Those conversations, his insights, and his unflagging friendship since those first days in Baton Rouge helped me immensely.

I owe an incalculable debt to two scholars who shaped how I approach history. During a National Endowment for the Humanities summer seminar titled "The Early American Republic and the Problem of Governance," Michael A. Morrison patiently worked me through the process of revising the manuscript for my first book. At the same time, the conversations we shared during that summer helped spark the idea that became this book. I miss him and his friendship greatly. Since 2005, William J. Cooper Jr., has shaped my development as a historian. First as a teacher and mentor and now as a friend,

Bill has taken interest in and unfailingly supported my work. His legacy as a scholar and teacher continues to shape how I strive to write and teach about American history.

Johns Hopkins University Press has taken excellent care of my work. Bob Brugger showed interest in my idea to write on the Webster-Hayne Debate, and after his retirement Elizabeth Demers and Lauren Straley steered the manuscript toward publication. George Roupe has been a model copyeditor. I am especially thankful to Peter Charles Hoffer and Williamjames Hull Hoffer, editors of the Witness to History series, for their support of this idea and their insights on several key ways to improve the book.

As much as I love being a historian, I love being a husband and father even more. My wife, Leah, and my three daughters, Elyse, Bridget, and now Jennifer, are the greatest blessing of all. To them, I dedicate this book.

Though the people acknowledged above have helped in making this book, it is mine and I accept full responsibility for it.

THE WEBSTER-HAYNE DEBATE

PROLOGUE

We the States or We the People?

DANIEL WEBSTER HAD A FULL AGENDA for himself on January 19, 1830. The forty-eight-year-old senator from Massachusetts, who maintained a law practice in addition to his duties as a senator, had business in the US Supreme Court one floor below the Senate chamber. Webster's tastes had always exceeded the income he earned as a senator, so representing wealthy patrons at the bar provided a much-welcomed supplemental income. During the morning, Webster attended to his case—a property dispute between the millionaire John Jacob Astor and the State of New York—in the court's crypt-like chambers in the ground level of the Capitol building. The room, claustrophobic with its low-slung barrel vaults that supported the room above in which forty-eight senators represented the Union's twenty-four states, had cramped quarters for the lawyers arguing before the high court. Along the east wall sat seven chairs on a slightly raised platform, where the justices of John Marshall's court presided over oral arguments.

Webster sat through deliberations during the morning, but once his work had ended, he wandered upstairs to the Senate chamber to follow its proceedings. The day had grown late; the Senate remained in session debating a resolution by Connecticut senator Samuel Augustus Foot to limit the sale of public lands to those parcels already on the market and to abolish the office of surveyor general of the public lands. The resolution, which Foot introduced several weeks earlier, had provoked lively debate between westerners who opposed the proposal and mistrusted his motives and northeasterners who supported efforts to slow the breakneck pace of westward expansion. Now in the afternoon hours, a southerner, Robert Young Hayne of South Carolina, rose to offer his remarks on the Foot resolution.

The Senate chamber in 1830 mirrored the shape of the Supreme Court's quarters below but felt much less confining and looked far more august. Forty-eight desks sat in semicircular rows facing east toward an elaborately decorated rostrum where the vice president of the United States—in 1830, John Caldwell Calhoun of South Carolina—presided over the legislative body in his role as president of the Senate. At the end of each aisle sat shiny brass spittoons that received frequent use; on the rail at the foot of the rostrum sat tiny snuffboxes from which senators could take a pinch during the course of debate. Perched above the crimson-draped presider's chair rested a gilt bald eagle poised to fly west from the rostrum. Behind a glass partition, senators could relax in a small gallery while still being able to hear the proceedings on the other side. Galleries encircled the room so that the people could observe their representatives at work. Eight Ionic columns of gray Potomac River marble supported the men's gallery above the rostrum. Women could observe from a semicircular gallery made of delicately adorned wrought iron. Below the women's gallery, a mahogany-paneled half wall separated the senators from privileged guests who could sit on sofas along the back wall. Light beamed from an ornate oil chandelier above as well as a large semicircular skylight in the coffered ceiling, surrounded by five smaller circular skylights. The room, by design, resembled the amphitheaters of old, where Roman and Grecian solons debated with one another.

As Webster, court papers under his arm, walked into the room and strode across the crimson wool carpet to his desk, he spied Senator Hayne, an intelligent but haughty member of the Palmetto State's elite ruling class, delivering his speech on the Foot resolution. Hayne stood in the well of the chamber facing east and addressing the presiding officer, his political mentor and friend Calhoun. Hayne had begun his speech by addressing the public lands issue and finding common cause with his western colleagues on the problems inherent in Foot's resolution. Then the senator let loose with a passionate defense of states' rights. "I am one of those who believe that the very life of our system is the independence of the States," Hayne argued, "and that there is no evil more to be more deprecated than the consolidation of this Government."[1] The senator continued his remarks by attacking what he saw as the purpose of Foot and the northeasterners: consolidation of the Union at the expense of states' rights.

Hayne intentionally broached a subject that had vexed Americans since their nation's genesis. Had the founders created a confederacy of sovereign states, or had they created a federal union governed by a central authority? Hayne believed the former. The states themselves had created the Union; they had granted it power in a few very specific instances and reserved the remainder of their sovereignty to themselves. Consolidation, or centralizing power in the federal government, meant a loss of independence, a loss of autonomy at a time when Hayne's home state of South Carolina and even the South itself needed most to guard its political and economic autonomy against outside interference. Threats to slavery and the southern economy abounded in the minds of Hayne and his fellow southerners.

We the *states* or we the *people*? Webster believed the latter, and Hayne's philippic against consolidation roused him to defend his own conception of the Union. The Senate adjourned after Hayne concluded his speech, but some of Webster's friends gathered round him to discuss the South Carolinian's remarks. "I did not like it, and my friends liked it less," Webster recalled several months later.[2] To a person, they voiced their opposition to Hayne's remarks on states' rights and pleaded with Webster to respond. In fact, the Massachusetts senator had sought an opportunity to defend his version of the Union against the radical states' rights doctrine that some southerners had embraced over the course of the 1820s. Now Webster had his opportunity.

During the evening, Webster pored over notes of his old speeches and writings and began to assemble a reply to Robert Hayne that he planned to deliver the next morning. Let Hayne rail about the ills of consolidation; Webster would strike back with a speech on the blessings of nationalism. Confident in his preparation, Webster strode to Capitol Hill the next morning with speech in hand and dressed for the occasion. For major speeches, Webster donned what observers called his oratorical costume—blue brass-buttoned coat, buff-colored vest, starched white shirt with cravat. The dress accentuated his appearance. Webster stood five feet ten inches and weighed approximately two hundred pounds—an imposing size in his day but not overpowering by any means. His striking physical features, however, distinguished him from all others. Webster had dark, deep-set eyes and bushy eyebrows that accentuated the piercing look that he gave to his audience. His black hair, slightly receding, stood in a shock on top of his large head, in no small part because Webster had a habit of running his hand across the top of his head when speaking. And then came the voice, that hypnotic voice as so many observers described his speaking. As an orator, Webster slowly built on his performance to the point that "all his faculties expand or take on a new character." The voice changed in tone to accentuate certain points; the black eyes flashed with force as he spoke. The entire performance, from the "angelical" smile to the "diabolical" scowl, enraptured the audience.[3]

And so Daniel Webster, momentarily to become known as defender of the Union, entered the Senate chamber on January 20, 1830, to do battle with Robert Hayne, opponent of consolidation and expositor of the baneful doctrine of states' rights. The Webster-Hayne Debate had commenced.

1

New England's March toward Nationalism

"IT WILL BE THE SOLEMN DUTY of the State Governments to protect their own authority over their own militia, and to interpose between their citizens and arbitrary power." The words came not from a southern nullifier in 1832 but from a New England Federalist in December 1814, in opposition to a bill providing for the conscription of soldiers into federal service. The southern nullifiers, those who in 1832 called for interposing against the federal tariff law and threatened secession over the issue, are often remembered for their stand against federal power. The New Englanders who belonged to the Federalist Party in 1814, as the Hartford Convention met to discuss its own version of nullification and even a veiled threat of secession, likewise saw state power as their only defense against majority power. Like many New England Federalists, this thirty-two-year-old congressman from New Hampshire looked at the War of 1812 as the ruin of his section and its interests. The embargo and the war had crippled the region's commerce and had caused a steep economic decline. The congressman, who had taken his seat in the House chamber only nine months earlier, had criticized the War Hawks throughout his young political career. The southerners and westerners who called for war to defend America's honor and sovereignty against the British menace—men like Henry Clay of Kentucky and John C. Calhoun of

South Carolina—saw nothing of the economic ruin that war would bring to New England's citizens, let alone the peril of taking on the formidable British military machine. Acting Secretary of War James Monroe floated several proposals for conscription to counteract the decline of able-bodied men ready for service. The martial spirit that had led many men to serve in the military against Great Britain had subsided amid a series of costly tactical blunders, while in New England a number of citizens protested the war by declining to serve and refusing to aid the American war effort. The debate over conscription seemed to turn the political world upside down; Jeffersonian Republicans justified the Monroe plan by invoking Alexander Hamilton's expansive definition of implied powers, while Federalists argued for strict construction of the Constitution. The young New Hampshire representative who rallied behind his New England colleagues, arguing that the Republicans had "libeled, foully libeled" the Constitution by proposing conscription, was Daniel Webster.[1]

Webster went beyond mere invective, however, by arguing that the states might have to interpose against the "unconstitutional and illegal" conscription measures should they become law. Webster's colleagues, deliberating in temporary quarters constructed after British soldiers had torched the Capitol building four months earlier, had to note the incongruity of this young Federalist upholding the principles of Thomas Jefferson and James Madison's Kentucky and Virginia Resolutions of 1798, in which the authors of the Declaration of Independence and the Constitution of 1787 had urged citizens in those states to repudiate the Alien and Sedition Acts. Though Madison called for the states to issue a solemn protest against laws viewed as unconstitutional by the states, Jefferson suggested that a state could nullify a federal law. Thirty years later, the nullifiers would draw inspiration from the Kentucky and Virginia Resolutions, much to the displeasure of the still-living James Madison. Perhaps Webster made the same observation, for even though he had drafted the speech for publication, he chose not to submit it to the House reporter for inclusion in the record. A generation later, when the nullifiers pored over the records of Webster's past for some hint of his alliance with the fractious New England Federalists, they somehow missed Webster's December 9 speech. That suited Webster, who for his part made sure that the speech did not make it into the *Annals of Congress* when congressional reporters Joseph Gales and William Seaton compiled their record of the Thirteenth Congress in the 1830s.[2]

Massachusetts senator Daniel Webster in 1831, just after he had engaged in the debate with Robert Hayne. His defense of nationalism cemented his status as an American statesman and helped to erase the stigma of New England sectionalism that had plagued his section since the War of 1812. Courtesy of the Library of Congress. Reproduction Number LC-DIG-pga-11871

Within days of Webster's address in the House of Representatives, a cabal of disgruntled Federalists met in Hartford, Connecticut, to calculate the value of the Union to the New England states. Though Webster had repudiated the notion of disunion in his speech to the House, his sympathies lay with those who sought to distance New England from the war and from the Republican policies that had proven ruinous to their section. Fortunately for Webster and those who participated in the Hartford Convention, moderates prevailed over the radicals, who loosely discussed creating a New England Confederacy. Instead the convention demanded a series of constitutional amendments that would protect the mercantile minorities of New England against the policies of southerners and westerners. They called for repeal of the three-fifths compromise, which to their minds had given the southern states outsized power in Congress by counting enslaved people as three-fifths of a person for purposes of taxation and representation. The convention's delegates also proposed a supermajority vote for the admission of new states to the Union, the passage of embargo legislation, and the declaration of war. Other amendments sought to prevent southern domination of the presidency and to enact term limits. The reactionary Hartford proposals reflected the fears and concerns of a section that saw itself as besieged by forces beyond its control. New Englanders feared westward expansion that would siphon off population from the Atlantic seaboard states. The embargoes enacted under the Jefferson and Madison administrations had withered the New England economy. War had led to persistent economic ruin. And it all had happened under the watch of Virginia Dynasty presidents who, according to the New England Federalists, had placed sectional supremacy over national interest. So they fought back by advancing their own agenda that would restore New England to glory.

The Hartford Convention's proposals were hardly as radical as some Federalists wanted or some Republicans claimed, but the perception of what had occurred at the convention irreparably damaged the Federalists' reputation in the nation. After the stunning victory of General Andrew Jackson's forces at the Battle of New Orleans and the war's end as negotiated in the Treaty of Ghent, an ebullient nationalism swept across the nation, a nationalism that made the dissenters at Hartford appear small, petty, and even disloyal. Within half a decade, the Federalist Party faded into irrelevance, the radical New Englanders bore the stigma of disunion, and the remainder of the old party's members, including young Daniel Webster, fought to distance themselves from the disgrace of secessionism that had poisoned the memory of the Hartford Convention.[3]

In her 1832 book, *Domestic Manners of the Americans*, the British novelist and writer Frances Trollope noted the intense tension between nationalism and regionalism in the United States. She never quite figured out the American predilection toward nation building on the one hand and parochialism on the other. Truth be told, neither had many Americans. The boundless self-confidence that Americans possessed exasperated Trollope. They knew that Providence had called them to a mission and that they possessed the wherewithal to accomplish the task, but they could not agree on what course to take. That final point would come to divide the nation in the early republic, making the grand plans for national unity elusive. From the vantage point of 1815, however, Trollope's concerns would have seemed out of place. Americans had miraculously freed themselves from British tyranny on the high seas; now they had to continue the process of liberation by building a stronger nation.[4]

The young United States had learned many lessons from its poor handling of the War of 1812. Given the course of the war itself, the American ministers signing the treaty in Ghent, Belgium, at Christmastime in 1814 must have felt fortunate indeed that its terms restored *status quo antebellum*. Americans after the war seemed more committed to building a stronger nation that united the sections of the Union. After all, New England's vehement dissent from the embargo and the war had illustrated the tensions inherent in the American nation. The mercantile New England states felt alienated from the agrarian South and West. Westward expansion had only exacerbated the underlying issues that divided Americans in the different sections of the Union. The question became evident at war's end: how could the nation knit the sections together into a coherent and coexistent whole?

In the war's aftermath, a cadre of political leaders believed they had found the answer to the troublesome question of national unity. They sought to craft an economic nationalism that would lead the United States forward into an expanding and evolving market economy. Their ideas revolved around three interlocking strategies that would become known by the end of the decade as the American System—the name given by Henry Clay of Kentucky. Economic nationalists like Clay endorsed a protective tariff to aid fledgling American industries, a national bank that would regulate the economic and monetary system, and a program for infrastructure development known at the time as internal improvements. Put together, the strategy would strengthen a nation whose weaknesses the War of 1812 had laid bare for the world to see.

Nearly forty years after the United States declared its independence from Great Britain, American industrial development languished. Manufacturing occurred chiefly in the home, where families produced goods for sale at market. Certain developments, like the slowly emerging textile mills of New England, seemed to promise a brighter future, but industrial growth moved slowly and haltingly. Finance plagued the nation's economy. The war had proven the folly of Congress's failure to renew the charter of the Bank of the United States. Alexander Hamilton's creation had provided the blueprint for a stable monetary system, but one year before war commenced between the United States and Great Britain, a divided Congress had narrowly voted to allow the bank's charter to expire. Jeffersonians had long harbored misgivings about the constitutionality of a national bank. Ordinary Americans feared the Philadelphia institution's far-reaching power over state and local banks. "It is a splendid association of favored individuals, taken from the mass of society, and invested with exemptions and surrounded by immunities and privileges," Kentucky senator Henry Clay caustically argued in the days before he became a proponent of national banking.[5] To the average American not conversant in the particulars of high finance, the Bank of the United States looked like a potential threat to individual liberty instead of a necessary regulator of America's crude and bewildering monetary system. The president had remained silent on the issue, knowing that Congress was closely divided on the recharter question. Vice President George Clinton's tiebreaking vote against renewal sealed the fate of the bank. The Jeffersonian agrarians killed the Federalist creation, but they soon rued their decision. Southerners and westerners alike found the scarcity of credit during and after the War of 1812 crippling to economic development. Clay and his allies called for a new bank. Finally, many of the same southerners and westerners who opposed national banking called for federal assistance for building roads, bridges, and canals that would aid in the transfer of raw materials from agricultural regions to urban centers. Internal improvements marked the most visible and tangible effort to knit the nation together by facilitating transportation and commerce.

The improvers hailed from across the United States. Clay, the spokesman for the developing West, typified his region's settlers. Born in Virginia just nine months after America had declared its independence, Clay became a student of the law and politics. In 1797, he moved to Kentucky, where he quickly became involved in local politics. Twice appointed to the US Senate, Clay found his greatest fame when he became a congressman at age thirty-four and then, astonishingly, Speaker of the House of Representatives. Here, amid of ongoing debate over the recurrent strife with Great Britain, Clay made his name as a War Hawk, one of the proponents of declaring war against the old mother country. Great Britain, according to the War Hawks, still held America in its clutches in a sort of quasi-colonial status. The British navy had violated American shipping, and the British soldiers stationed across the northern border of the United States—and even within American territory— had incited Indian resistance and rebellion. The United States had to assert

Henry Clay of Kentucky, about 1822. At the time of the Webster-Hayne Debate, the proponent of the American System had already served as a representative, Speaker of the House, senator, and secretary of state. The year after the debate, Clay would return to the Senate. Courtesy of the Library of Congress. Reproduction Number LC-USZ62-5083

its sovereignty, but autonomy meant nothing without the wherewithal to enjoy its benefits. At war's end, Clay began to develop the economic system that became synonymous with his name thereafter.

Clay authored the American System, but he had support from politicians throughout the nation. Another wunderkind, John Caldwell Calhoun of South Carolina, likewise became a spokesman for economic nationalism. Five years younger than Clay, Calhoun joined Clay in the Twelfth Congress as a representative from a low-country district where planters produced rice and indigo with the labor of enslaved Africans. After the war, Calhoun became a powerful defender of economic nationalism and a critic of narrow-minded regionalism. With his piercing eyes directed northeast, the young congressman lamented that one section of the nation seemed willing to forgo the benefits of economic and political nationalism to all for a narrower vision of union. To his mind, Americans of all regions must unite behind a strong transportation system and a nationally coordinated economy.

Two slightly older leaders joined young Clay and Calhoun in the quest for national unity. Both John Quincy Adams of Massachusetts and Andrew Jackson of Tennessee supported the nationalist program as the best means of securing the nation's economic independence. Westerners like Jackson clamored for internal improvements that could connect the hinterlands to eastern markets. Northeasterners like Adams desired the boom in commerce that would come with better roads and water routes. In sum, the improvers believed that commercial, agricultural, and manufacturing interests would all benefit from national planning. Indeed, they saw America's national security and the people's liberty preserved and secured by their program of mutual uplift.

President James Madison, having felt the sting of war all too closely, likewise endorsed a nationalist program in his 1815 annual message to Congress. Writing from a townhouse three blocks from the burned-out shell of the Executive Mansion, Madison dispatched a message to Congress that embodied the postwar spirit.[6] In the message, the president endorsed the program of the economic nationalists: a national bank, a tariff, and internal improvements, though he expressed doubts that the Constitution would allow the latter without amendment. Some observers argued that Madison had appropriated Alexander Hamilton's system of political economy by advocating such a nationalist agenda. True, chartering another national bank would resurrect Hamilton's original scheme for regulating the national economy and marked a significant shift in the Republican Party platform. Madison had avoided the debate, though Albert Gallatin, his secretary of the treasury, had tried in vain to secure the recharter.

Madison correctly read the postwar mind-set of Americans who wanted to lay aside parochial squabbles and embark on a program of national economic development, and so he led the Republicans toward a program in which many Federalists would have found little to oppose. Madison explained the obvious economic and military benefits that would stem from his agenda, but he also emphasized that the tripartite plan would serve the nation by "binding together the various parts of our extended confederacy," a notion that became the foundation of Clay's American System.[7] The hardships of war had led Madison to reconsider—at least partially—his inclinations toward Jeffersonian simplicity in government. The president intended to undertake, with a cooperative Congress, measures to strengthen the fabric of the Union that the Republicans of a decade earlier would have viewed suspiciously. "However wise the theory may be which leaves to the sagacity and interest of individuals the application of their industry and resources," Madison wrote in his annual message, "there are in this as in other cases exceptions to the general rule."[8] Madison's program, to many observers, was a significant exception to the Republican rule indeed.

In many ways, though, Madison's shift reflected the attitudes of Americans who had suffered from the travails of uncoordinated political economy during the War of 1812. In the fall of 1814, Americans had elected the Fourteenth Congress, an extraordinary assemblage of leaders of whom a majority supported vigorous national action. Two of the nationalist War Hawks would return to Congress when it reconvened in December 1815; Clay again as Speaker of the House and Calhoun as chairman of the House Committee on National Currency. Clay led the nationalists in the proactive House, while Calhoun acted as the floor manager, securing support for critical votes and ensuring that the nationalist platform sailed through the chamber. Both encouraged a broad interpretation of the Constitution, even more expansive than Madison had envisioned, that would allow for national economic development.

Not everyone believed that the agenda coming out of Congress would preserve liberty and protect the nation. A group of Virginians emerged in opposition to economic nationalism on the grounds that the federal government had no authority to intervene and interfere in the economy. The Old Republicans, champions of states' rights and strict construction of the Constitution, urged restraint. Men like John Randolph, the eccentric, diminutive congressman from Roanoke County, Virginia, shrill in voice and opinion, opposed the president's plans on the grounds that the government would grow bloated in size and the taxpayers would have to foot the bill. When Calhoun introduced the bank bill in January 1816, Randolph objected on constitutional grounds. "The question is whether or not we are willing to become one great consolidated nation, under one form of law; whether the state governments are to be swept away; or whether we have still respect enough for those old, respectable institutions to regard their integrity and preservation as part of our policy."[9] Hearkening back to the Jeffersonian conception of the nation as an agrarian republic, Randolph forcefully opposed efforts to assist in the development of a merchant and manufacturing class. But since the war, politics had transcended the old debates between the Hamiltonians and Jeffersonians on the nature of the republic.

The planter class in Virginia wondered if the president, one of their own after all, had taken leave of his good senses. As the influential John Taylor of Caroline (as he was known, of Caroline County, Virginia) argued, an alliance between commerce and the government would produce a commercial aristocracy that would hold the farmers and planters of the nation in a state of fealty. A protective tariff, for example, would destroy the agrarian economy by decreasing demand for American agricultural surpluses while raising the price on imports on which the agrarians depended. Ensuring economic and political liberty required the government to abstain from interference; the American System, according to Taylor and his contemporaries, instead placed the government in the position of choosing favorites. In the April 1824 debate over a survey bill for roads and canals, Taylor argued that certain interest groups, "dictated by local interest or prejudice," ignored strict construction of the Constitution for the benefit of the few. Public welfare required a narrow construction of the Constitution's grant of implied powers to the federal government, "leaving individuals, partnerships, and States, as much as possible to pursue their own interest, in their own way." A Congress committed to strict construction provided the "only good evidence that the Government is founded in reason and justice, and not in error and fraud."[10]

The Virginians found allies in North Carolina, where economic conditions mirrored those of the Old Dominion. The agrarians of both states equated postwar economic nationalism with the resurgence of Hamiltonian Federalism, a fearful specter that threatened mid-Atlantic power and domination. The vicissitudes of agriculture had left farmers and planters in both states wary of their future. Talk of a protective tariff that would cut into the increasingly elusive wealth of tobacco country made agriculturalists clutch their pocketbooks ever tighter. Meanwhile, the mid-Atlantic states shared New England fears of the accelerating westward expansion. The farmers migrating to western states in search of greater opportunity and fresher soils led Virginians in particular to fear the loss of their political influence. In a state that counted three of the first four presidents as favorite sons, any diminution of political power at the federal level threatened the Old Dominion's supremacy in federal politics.

The Old Republicans were not the only ones who feared for their political and economic future. The new Madisonian Republicanism left Federalists like Daniel Webster in a quandary. Webster, the gifted lawyer who parleyed his brilliant oratorical skills into a political career, emerged as a leading Federalist at a time when the party faced imminent collapse. The Republicans, many Federalists observed, had co-opted the Federalist economic agenda after having fought against it for almost two decades. Madison's call for rechartering the Bank of the United States seized the attention of Federalists who quickly pointed out that leading Republicans had opposed the policy before the war had commenced. The Republicans, remarked one wry Bostonian, "are now, good souls, heartily in love with a national bank. A lover never sighed half so much for his absent fair-one, as they have within the year for the establishment of a bank."[11] On the other hand, the Republicans' apparent embrace of the Federalist position on political economy blurred the lines between parties and further accelerated the decline of Federalism in American politics. Moreover, any hope of inaugurating an actual Era of Good Feelings proved impossible with the continued Republican misgivings toward Federalist politicians, especially those who had questioned the war or, more gravely, endorsed the Hartford Convention.

Between 1815 and 1825, the New England Federalists joined their Virginia colleagues in opposition to key elements of the American System. Both viewed transportation improvements with a mixture of cynicism and short-sightedness. Ignoring the potential long-term economic benefits of strengthened internal trade routes, Virginians and New Englanders withheld support for internal improvements that required expenditures beyond their confines. Why build better roads and waterways that would only serve to allow the residents of their respective sections to move west with greater ease? Both regions maintained an Atlantic orientation at a time when the nation's future seemed headed toward the Mississippi. New England clung to its British mercantile connections, while Virginia remained dependent on foreign markets for its tobacco crop. The West, to both regions, drained the East of people and other needed economic resources.

The tariff proved equally problematic to different regions within the Union for different reasons. The postwar tariff of 1816 enjoyed broad support across sectional lines through Congress, though it failed to achieve its desired goal of shielding American industries from the onslaught of inexpensive British imports that flooded the American market. British manufactures hailed the return of the export trade that would boost their economy; the government likewise saw a benefit in keeping Americans dependent on British manufactures. Many Americans saw the problem of British dependency, but they could not agree on how to respond. By the early 1820s, the significant economic differences between different sections of the nation stymied efforts to create an economic system that all Americans could support. Instead, each section sprang to the defense of its unique circumstances, making the discussion of economic nationalism a divisive issue. An "Era of Good Feelings," of hopes for economic integration, of dreams for a system that united American farmers, merchants, and manufacturers behind a common banner, succumbed to sectional self-interest.

After the failure of the 1816 tariff to aid American industry against British imports, a coalition of westerners called for higher duties on an array of foreign imports. Kentuckians blamed their sluggish hemp market on the British, while Ohio River valley producers could not compete against British glass and other products. Meanwhile, southern planters faced a different sort of pressure: amid falling prices for agricultural staples they spoke against any measure that would increase taxes. And because the South relied on the British import market, they opposed tariffs that they believed would provoke costly economic retaliation. When Congress considered a new tariff eight years later, new fault lines on the tariff issue had emerged. The South opposed the tariff while the mid-Atlantic states, the residents of the Ohio River valley, and the Northwest voted in favor of protection.

New England Federalists who held a strong commitment to mercantile interests found Madison's call for a protective tariff hard to embrace. Their region had not yet experienced the transformation to manufacturing that would soon come and would lead politicians toward protectionism. After the War of 1812, enterprising Republicans sought to build political capital, especially in the commercial states, by calling for tariffs that would protect emerging home industries. Meanwhile, the declining Federalists seemed too wedded to free trade to recognize the immense benefits that protectionism would bring to the budding manufacturing industry. They held stubbornly to the beliefs of an older generation that had amassed wealth via maritime shipping instead of home industries. The New England economy, however, was in the midst of rapid and consequential change as the Industrial Revolution expanded within the United States.

The development of textile mills in New England during the early 1820s and beyond made the old Federalist hostility toward protection obsolete. What started with a small group of Rhode Island merchants backing a young British immigrant's efforts to develop a textile mill in 1789 blossomed into a profitable industry that ushered in a new era and a new economy. Samuel Slater's cotton mill offered a prototype for the kind of industry that New England could support. Advances in American manufacturing led New England's mercantile interests toward the development of a textile industry that would come to dominate the region's economy within a decade. Economically speaking, New England's growth as a manufacturing region stemmed from the constraints of geography and from sound logic. Northeastern soils would never support intensive agriculture; meanwhile, the section's longstanding presence as a maritime economy led naturally to an expansion of manufacturing. New England could easily and efficiently ship the goods it produced. Burgeoning manufacturers from the region, however, simply could not survive without a tariff to shield them from British competition. The looms of New England produced a cloth inferior to the refined products of Great Britain's mills, and in the aftermath of the war British textile manufacturers flooded the American markets with cloth in an effort to force American manufacturers out of business. By 1820, then, New Englanders had begun to embrace the idea of protectionism as the means by which their textile industries would grow in the face of stiff competition from Great Britain.

Alexander Hamilton had dreamt of the kind of industrial development that emerged in New England during the 1820s, but the process of creating viable manufacturing in the United States took a generation. Even Thomas Jefferson, who during his presidency had fought to maintain the idyllic agrarian republic of his dreams, had converted to the cause of economic nationalism by the end of the 1810s. "To be independent for the comforts of life Americans must fabricate these for themselves," Jefferson argued in 1816. "We must now place the manufacturer by the side of the agriculturalist."[12] Economic independence, however, required capital and expertise, something that American manufacturing lacked in its early years. Dozens of men like Samuel Slater had to prove not only that Americans could evolve beyond home industries but also that they could compete with British industry.

Between 1810 and 1825, the evolution of American manufacturing progressed as innovations in manufacturing and transportation, plus the influx of capital, allowed for industrial growth. The Market Revolution, as historians have described this rapid period of manufacturing and commercial development in the early republic, had commenced. With the emergence of the Market Revolution more Americans became integrated within the business cycle and more responsive to concerns regarding banking, interstate trade, and regional economics. The Market Revolution integrated Americans into a larger economy that often seemed distant and impersonal but that also had a significant impact on their daily lives. Consequently, economic issues became central to American politics in the years following the War of 1812.

The revolution started in places like Waltham, Massachusetts, where in 1811 a Boston merchant named Francis Cabot Lowell devised a plan to construct a mill to produce cotton cloth. Lowell needed three things at the outset of his venture: machinery, capital, and organization. With assistance from a mechanic who had knowledge of British textile manufacturing, Lowell designed a power loom that would allow for large-scale production of cotton cloth. With the machinery designed, Lowell began to solicit investors among his merchant friends for the development of the mill. Finally, Lowell asked the Massachusetts state legislature for a corporate charter for the Boston Manufacturing Company, which gave the company legal status and protection under the law. The process took a decade to complete, but by 1822, the Boston Associates, the group of investors behind Waltham, chose to develop a second mill at a town wholly created for the purpose of manufacturing textiles. The company town had been born. Together, the original mill at Waltham and the second site at the town of Lowell transformed American industry by using the best technology available, placing all elements of production within one site and utilizing the inexpensive labor of local people, including young farm women desperate to try something besides agriculture. In Massachusetts, the transportation, industrial, and market revolutions converged in a way that changed American commerce forever. Their investment required a reconceived political economy that would allow industry to mature.[13]

The interests of New England industrialists meshed with the platform of the man who won the presidency in 1824. John Quincy Adams, son of the second president, envisioned a program of national development even grander than the American System that would secure New England's destiny and bind the nation together. In what one historian of the era has termed the "climactic document of Republican nationalism," Adams outlined a plan for national economic development aided by an activist government.[14] The president, a Massachusetts native himself, endorsed tariffs as part of his bold plan of national economic development. In his first annual message to Congress, Adams wholeheartedly endorsed the American System, even as he embellished it beyond the dreams of its chief proponent, Henry Clay, who joined the Adams administration as secretary of state. Adams called for an impressive program of internal improvements designed to facilitate commerce and transportation and coordinated at the federal level, an astonishing proposal well ahead of its time. In general, Adams proposed to use revenue from the sale of western lands to finance the construction of roads and canals that would connect the nation. He endorsed the tariff not as a revenue generator but as a means of supporting the growth and development of American industry. His more daring proposals called for the erection of a national observatory, the creation of a national university, and the addition of a Department of the Interior to the executive branch.

Adams surely understood the audacity of his proposals, for even as he expressed his sincere belief that they would serve to bind the nation together and create a national economy that could sustain American liberty and prosperity, he also addressed the inevitable constitutional challenges that would come from the proponents of limited government. The response to Adams's annual message did indeed indicate that the Era of Good Feelings had come to a close and that the Republicans had irreparably divided into two factions: the nationalists and the states' rights particularists. He did not, however, understand his audience. Adams took the impolitic step of lecturing Congress on the correct interpretation of the Constitution's delegation of powers to the federal government. More perilously, he intimated to the legislators that democracy and popular sovereignty could go too far. "The spirit of improvement is abroad upon the earth," Adams counseled the Nineteenth Congress, and "were we to slumber in indolence or fold up our arms and proclaim to the world that we are palsied by the will of our constituents, would it not be to cast away the bounties of Providence and doom ourselves to perpetual inferiority?"[15]

Adams erred, however, by writing an opening address that read as if he had achieved a mandate through a decisive election. The circumstances of his election proved the contrary. In four years, American presidential politics went from having an uncontested election that handed James Monroe a second term to an election in which four men vied for the high office. Factionalism had hearkened the end of the Era of Good Feelings. James Monroe's quaint dream of a nation without parties gave way to myriad factions that loosely mirrored the different sections of the Union. All four candidates called themselves Democratic-Republicans, but party unity failed absent competition from the Federalists. From the West, Henry Clay and Andrew Jackson tossed their hats into the ring. Friends of the congressional nominating caucus selected William Crawford of Georgia, but the antidemocratic method of selecting a nominee seemed increasingly anachronistic in the changed politics of the era. Adams drew support from New York and the New England states. Jackson won a plurality of the popular vote; indeed, he was the only candidate to gain significant support beyond his section. Winning 41.4 percent of the popular vote, Jackson bested the eventual winner John Quincy Adams by 10.5 percent.

Because no candidate secured a majority vote in the Electoral College, however, the House of Representatives had to select the new president according to the provisions of the Twelfth Amendment. The top three vote takers competed in the contingent election, leaving Speaker of the House Clay out of the running. The real contest, however, was between Adams and Jackson. Crawford had suffered a debilitating stroke during the election, which largely ended his candidacy. Henry Clay, jilted by the electorate, now emerged as a powerful figure given his role as Speaker of the House. Bitter and furious, Clay derided the people's choice, Andrew Jackson. "I cannot believe that killing 2,500 Englishmen at New Orleans qualifies for the various, difficult, and complicated duties of the Chief Magistracy," he thundered.[16] After securing assurances from Adams that he would support the American System if elected president, Clay worked behind the scenes to gain votes for the Massachusetts native. On February 9, 1825, Adams won the presidency and nominated Clay as his secretary of state. Now Jackson railed against a corrupt bargain between the president and his secretary of state, Clay, whom he likened to Judas Iscariot. The election of 1828 began on the day the House of Representatives decided the election of 1824. In the intervening four years, partisan rancor reached new heights as Jackson supporters rallied behind their man to avenge the corruption that had led to an Adams presidency. So when Adams outlined a strategy for national economic development during his first days in office, he did so with no political strength.

In the aftermath of the bitterly contested election, it became clear that Adams had hardly received a mandate from the electorate, and his advisors knew it. During a discussion between Adams and his cabinet on a draft of the message, Henry Clay wryly noted, "We seem to be stripping off your draft alternately." Adams replied, "It's like the man with two wives. One is plucking out his white hairs, the other the black, until none are left."[17] The president's own cabinet had warned him to temper his agenda and language; the American people, they argued would not yet accept such an ambitious program of economic nationalism. In a country where people rarely encountered the federal government in their day-to-day lives except for the delivery of mail, the use of federal power and national treasure for such extravagances as a national university seemed insensible. Even in the headiest days of postwar nationalism, the electorate would have viewed such plans with skepticism. Yet in terms of Adams's more prosaic initiatives, such as investment in internal improvements, the president faced relatively little criticism from the public. Indeed, Adams and his advisors had designed the program carefully to assuage all sections; he proposed, for example, the construction of a national road from Washington, DC, to New Orleans to placate southern commercial interests and the completion of a canal connecting the Chesapeake Bay with the Ohio River as economic stimulus to the burgeoning West. In the end, however, Adams presented the entire plan as part of a grand agenda.

When criticism did come, it arrived from the disaffected congressional supporters of the men whom Adams bested in the election of 1824. The alliance of John Quincy Adams and Henry Clay drew fire not only from Andrew Jackson but also from the supporters of William Crawford and John C. Calhoun of South Carolina. The most direct attacks came from the Old Republicans, who viewed economic nationalism as suspicious at best and unconstitutional at worst. The plans for internal improvements, in the words of one of Adams's biographers, "only served to recall Patrick Henry's old fear of a Great Magnificent Government that would consolidate federal power into national power and do away with the reserved rights of the states."[18] They pilloried the president as an aristocrat who saw fit to ignore the will of the people. Criticism aside, Adams inaugurated a new era of federal involvement in economic expansion. By the second year of the Adams presidency, one historian has noted, "the federal government had become the largest entrepreneur in the American economy" through its support of internal improvements.[19]

Transformations in American politics and the peculiar circumstances surrounding Adams's ascendancy to the presidency doomed his administration from its outset. Adams could wax poetic about economic nationalism all he wished, he could lecture Congress about fulfilling its duties to the American people, but he could not achieve victory for his program because he had assumed the presidency under such extraordinary circumstances. The election of 1824 marked a transformation in American politics that itself exhibited that the body politic remained conflicted over economic nationalism and an overall vision for the future of the nation.

Between James Monroe's uncontested reelection to the presidency in 1820 to his retirement from public life four years later, the Era of Good Feelings in American politics disappeared. Congress grew more polarized among regional factions and interests that hardly bore the structure of party politics but that nonetheless had considerable influence on local and regional constituencies. Economic nationalism and the American System surely figured into the election, but the decline of the presidential nominating caucus also altered to the transforming political landscape. For twenty-eight years, the Republican Party had determined the nominee via a party caucus composed of congressmen. With the end of two-party politics, however, the caucus system seemed unnecessary. Necessity aside, the real complaint about the caucus system came from another product of the postwar era: the call for democracy in the American republic. A growing number of Americans scoffed at the notion that a caucus of party regulars had the power to choose a presidential nominee without consulting the electorate. "Caucuses are at a low ebb," New Hampshire politician William Plumer wrote in 1820 to his son who served in the House of Representatives. "They have, in general, discovered too much management and intrigue—too much regard for *private*, & too little respect for the *public interest*."[20] "King Caucus," as the proponents of democratic reform called the old system, perverted the notion of popular sovereignty. "King Numbers"—or the vote of the people—should determine the nominee.

The democratic impulse in American politics strengthened between 1817 and 1824, as three states opened suffrage to virtually all white men over the age of twenty-one by drastically reducing property requirements as an impediment to vote. Five more western states admitted to the Union during the same period never instituted property requirements in their constitutions. This state-level constitutional revolution changed the electorate by increasing its size. In turn, the involvement of more people in the political process brought changes in how states governed themselves. Public officials once appointed by governors or legislatures now had to stand for election. States that had reserved the selection of electors to the Electoral College now called for a popular vote for the president.

In the long term, democratization in American politics during the 1820s led to the creation of two relatively stable political parties that dominated between the 1830s and 1850s. In the short term, however, it created a chaotic situation in which four candidates competed for the presidency. Without a national party system, sophisticated organization and mobilization of voters could not happen. Each candidate seemed to court a particular region rather than develop a national coalition of supporters. Accordingly, industrializing New England and the northwestern states endorsed Adams. The Old Republicans of Virginia, wary of economic nationalism, endorsed native-born William Crawford. Henry Clay and his American System found support in the Ohio River valley, while Andrew Jackson carried the new southwestern states. A fifth candidate, John C. Calhoun, dropped out of the race and settled instead for the vice presidency when he failed to garner support outside of his native South Carolina.

Given the assemblage of personalities seeking the presidency in 1824, one might assume that the election revolved around people rather than issues. Admittedly, the magnetic Andrew Jackson commanded a strong following with his personality. The fear of corruption and the perceived loss of public virtue, however, played a critical role alongside visions of the future to give the election a deeper meaning. Fissures within the old Jeffersonian coalition had become apparent as the campaign devolved into a contest of regional loyalties. Moreover, the emergence of white man's democracy, as historians have labeled the expansion of the electorate in the early 1820s, fueled substantial discussions about politics during the election. Jackson emerged as the front-runner, inasmuch as any candidate could in a four-way race. His managers correctly sensed the spirit of democracy in the nation and portrayed Old Hickory as the exemplar of popular sovereignty. Supporters endorsed him as "a friend to the *rights of man* and *universal suffrage*," platitudes that played well on the frontier and even in more established regions of the Union.[21]

Courting the frontier vote had become important for politicians of all stripes, as the West grew in population and stature. The rise of manufacturing and commerce during the 1820s in New England and the northwestern states brought conflict over another important issue of the day: westward expansion. Though northerners sought to use economic nationalism to forge closer ties to the expanding western states and nascent territories, they generally had unfavorable views on expansion. Unrestrained geographic expansion, or expansion across space, they argued, threatened national stability and the greater good of developing the nation's existing land. Expansion through time, by improving the land the nation currently controlled, promised the greatest long-term economic and political benefits. Reckless speculation in western lands, which contributed to the Panic of 1819, led northeasterners to resist demands for cheap lands on the frontier. Moreover, the emerging business and manufacturing classes in New England believed that rapid westward migration would drain the Northeast of much-needed workers to fuel the development of the market economy. Consequently, calls from the South and West for westward expansion met resistance from northerners.

In the years following the War of 1812, the United States witnessed one of the most massive movements of people in its history, as thousands of settlers from the East traversed the Appalachian Mountains to settle in the interior beyond. By 1820, over two million Americans lived west of the mountains. They followed two major streams of migration. Residents of Georgia, Tennessee, North Carolina, and South Carolina migrated to the southwest, especially to the future states of Mississippi and Alabama, which gained admission to the Union in 1817 and 1819. The predominately Scotch-Irish population settled in the numerous alluvial river valleys of the two new states as well as in Louisiana, on the fertile west bank of the Mississippi River. There, these farmers sought to capitalize on the emerging cotton boom that brought unparalleled prosperity to the region, built on the labor of enslaved people. The second wave of migration led thousands more to the lands north of the Ohio River. The Old Northwest had seen settlement much earlier; the state of Ohio, for example, had been admitted to the Union in 1803. The postwar migration, however, transformed it into the fourth-most populous state in the Union by 1820. Settlers migrating from the Upper South filled in southern Ohio and formed new communities in the southern parts of two future states: Indiana and Illinois. In the northern portion of these three states, residents of New York and the New England states replicated on the western frontier the communities they had left behind back east.

The New Englanders who had settled in the Old Northwest tried their best to build a society like the one they had left behind. They developed a second wheat belt that rivaled that of New York and Pennsylvania, and by the 1820s, they used the Erie Canal to ferry their agricultural products back to eastern markets and merchants. These economic connections, forged at the moment when American manufacturing stood ready to transform the market economy, cemented ties between the upper midwestern states and their former neighbors in New England and New York. Economically and culturally they shared common affinities that bound them together well beyond the end of the postwar boom.

The great migrations after the War of 1812, however, came at a cost that many of those two million settlers who migrated beyond the Appalachians either did not discern or chose to ignore. With the rapid movement of so many Americans came a class of businessmen who earned their gains by rampant speculation in land. After all, eastern settlers only made the risky trip west because of the promise of fresh, fertile lands for farming. Speculation ran wild after the war, as absentee owners sought to claim the best lands and hold them for the day when rising land values allowed them to turn a tidy profit. Legitimate settlers resented their actions, but as historian Daniel Walker Howe has explained, the western settlers bore culpability in the land fever as well.[22] Farmers often bought more land than they could possibly cultivate on their own, in hope of realizing future profits on increasing land values. Boomtowns grew on the frontier of the Old Northwest as places where agriculturalists could engage in trade. Trade and stable communities connected to the hinterlands brought increased value to the lands that settlers had purchased at rock-bottom prices, courtesy of a liberal federal land policy that encouraged people to buy low in hopes of selling high. The real estate bubble expanded dramatically in the four years after the War of 1812 as the participants of the great westward migrations settled on the frontier.

Then came the seemingly inevitable burst of the bubble. Westerners had overextended themselves with credit based on the beliefs that Europe would continue to demand American agricultural products and that land prices would increase without interruption. Moreover, the federal government had implicitly encouraged the purchase of public lands on credit, which fed the speculative boom that ensued after the war. By 1818, the speculative fervor had reached a fever pitch as the rise of land prices accelerated, credit remained plentiful, and the prices of agricultural staples in international markets bordered on the irrational. In October of that year, cotton prices in Liverpool, England, reached the dizzying price of 32.5 cents a pound. By 1819, however, Europe had begun to recover from the disruptions wrought by the Napoleonic Wars. Cotton prices decreased by over half, credit tightened as banks called in loans and demanded payment in gold or silver, and the frontier became cash starved.

The cotton bust severely damaged the southern agricultural economy, but the western states suffered even more from the collapse of the land market and the tightening of credit on the frontier. Land sales plummeted so low that incoming revenues from sales could not meet the expenses of surveying and selling the lands. The constriction wiped out many families as westerners sold their property for pennies on the dollar. For the westerners who believed that they had merely followed the quintessentially American process of westward expansion, the Panic of 1819 proved a harsh rebuke to accept. They had moved west in hopes of building a future through their own labor only to find their dreams smashed by what seemed to them a distant and incomprehensible foe: the incomprehensible and fickle financial system.[23]

Many westerners blamed eastern financiers, particularly the Second Bank of the United States, headquartered in Philadelphia. Distant eastern bankers, the despondent westerners argued, had brought forth the collapse of the economy. They had contracted the money supply to a point that westerners scarcely had money to spend. The rapid drain of specie, gold and silver, and the removal of paper notes that the precious metals supposedly gave value to, had left the frontier without any means of credit. Not all westerners agreed, however, on how to remedy the problem. In Tennessee, the influential Andrew Jackson and gubernatorial candidate William Carroll sparred over how the state should react to the panic. Both men agreed that the banks had caused the economic downturn. But whereas Carroll, a hardware merchant whose business suffered greatly from the downturn, called for public relief for the indebted as a part of his campaign for governor, Jackson sided with a coalition of large landholders and merchants who opposed any measures that would harm creditors. Carroll won the 1820 election against opposition from Jackson and his followers, suggesting that many Tennesseans demanded some form of relief.[24] Others blamed the settlers themselves. Kentucky newspaper editor Amos Kendall argued, "*The people must pay their own debts at last. This truth should be impressed upon them, their eyes should be turned from banks and the legislature to themselves,—their own power and resources.*"[25]

The instability of the American monetary system in the antebellum era created an often wildly gyrating boom and bust cycle in which flush times would give way to extreme economic hardship characterized by the withdrawal of paper money from the economy. In the days before the federal government standardized a system of paper currency, American banks created the paper notes that allowed currency to flow through the economy. Individual states granted corporate status to these small banks, and then investors bought stock in the bank to provide the capital necessary to open for business. The banks then could issue loans to borrowers on demand, which they did in the form of paper notes that people could use to purchase their needs and wants. Theoretically, anyone who accepted the notes could redeem them for specie at the issuing bank.

True, this primitive system of currency exchange was better than a barter economy, but it nevertheless had serious flaws that led to the periodic collapse of the American market economy. First, the stockholders in a bank often pledged their investment via IOUs, a risky proposition that unscrupulous investors could often exploit. Second, banks could—and usually did—lend far more money than they held in gold and silver reserves. As long as a bank could meet the demand for converting notes to specie, the bank faced no difficulty. And as long as the economy remained solid and borrowers paid their loans back with the required interest, no one would notice. Unfortunately, the banks frequently overextended themselves by issuing credit too far in excess of their specie reserves. When hard times came and borrowers defaulted on their loans, a bank could easily exhaust its reserves. Moreover, if the investors in a bank could not pay their IOUs with specie, a bank could easily bankrupt itself. Inflation ensued, and a false sense of prosperity further fed the boom cycle, as the hyperinflated prices of cotton in 1818 illustrate. Inevitably, the bubble would burst, and inflation easily gave way to crippling deflation.

Perhaps the most dangerous part of the unstable banking system stemmed from the constantly changing value of bank-issued currency. A ten-dollar note from an Ohio bank, for example, would not necessarily buy ten dollars' worth of goods and services. Any merchant or bank could "discount" the value of the note based on numerous factors, such as the reputation of the bank's directors, its history of prudent fiscal strategy, or its capital reserves. Location trumped all other considerations in a monetary system that limited many transactions to the distance a bank's reputation carried. Few people were privy to such information; moreover, these variables often changed in a relatively brief time. For the ordinary merchant or farmer, the intricacies of banking proved impossible to master. But when someone accepted that ten-dollar note for payment, only to find out subsequently that the note was worthless, economic realities became very real.

During a panic, all of the flaws within the patchwork system of paper currency became apparent. When an economic downturn sapped the confidence of people holding bank currency, they naturally sought to redeem the money for specie. Conditions created a run on the banks, which could exhaust a firm's reserves rapidly. Typically, a bank would suspend the payment of specie by refusing to redeem notes for specie in an effort to stave off a complete collapse of reserves. The value of the paper notes plummeted, employers laid off workers, and deflation would set in as the money supply contracted. In some extreme circumstances, bartering would resume as a means of exchange. Banks resumed payment in specie only when those who had hoarded gold and silver chose to release their reserves into the economy. Then the cycle started again.[26]

In theory, the Bank of the United States served as a regulator of sorts within the convoluted system of American currency. With the US government as its biggest source of business—by statute, the BUS served as the federal government's official banker—the bank possessed unparalleled reserves that gave it far-reaching power over the thousands of smaller banks in the nation. The BUS could essentially hoard the notes of any smaller bank it suspected of fiscal malfeasance and then demand payment in specie, a prospect that would bankrupt the smaller bank. At the very least, the looming threat of such action could encourage smaller banks to adopt more judicious loan practices and encourage more substantial reserves. Because of a series of missteps by the BUS and its directors, however, the nation's largest bank ignored its congressional charge to promote sound monetary policy and instead focused on amassing profits for itself from the boom cycle. When the panic struck in 1819, the BUS had little control over the wildcat banks of the western states.[27]

With the Panic of 1819, Americans had their first experience of the violent business cycle that dominated antebellum American economics. The catastrophe illustrated not only the problems inherent in the American economic system but that the link between western agriculturalists and eastern merchants was stronger than perhaps either group cared to admit. Eastern merchants would feel the ripple effect of the credit crisis in the West; westerners felt the sting of falling prices. To many of the farmers ruined by the panic, the BUS had acted precipitously and arbitrarily to remedy its own problems. One wry observer captured the sentiment of many westerners: "The Bank was saved and the people were ruined."[28]

Though westerners saw the Philadelphia bank as the monster that had capriciously destroyed their livelihoods, the truth was more complex. Indeed, the main branch of the BUS had allowed loose credit on the frontier for far too long. Westerners and their banks had imbibed the loose flowing credit to a dangerous point and the BUS, which should have acted as a regulator against the speculation, failed to rein in the western land boom in time. The lack of urgency exacerbated the disastrous situation. The people and their representatives in Congress demanded answers and looked for where to lay the blame. Some blamed Congress itself for endorsing such a reckless land policy that had abetted speculation. New Englanders in particular fumed at western recklessness. But with the passage of the Land Act of 1820, by which Congress lowered the price of public land to $1.25 an acre and lowered the minimum purchase requirement to eighty acres, opponents argued that the legislators had doubled down on policies that favored speculation. Western-ers also blamed the government, in spite of the fact that Washington's liberal land policies had spurred expansion in the first place. Some called for the states to administer public land distribution, while others called for a reduc-tion in prices to foster the growth of the West as a place where honest yeomen could settle even if they could not pay the federally mandated prices.[29]

In sum, the postwar land boom and its subsequent collapse during the Panic of 1819 illustrated the significance of economic interests to the Ameri-can political system. As the Market Revolution brought home to many Ameri-cans the realities of the business cycle, one particular economic issue came to dominate discussions of political economy. Protective tariffs became a significant part of national politics during the decade as northeastern manu-facturers gradually abandoned their free-trade scruples in favor of a tariff for manufacturing. Protecting the infant American manufacturing sector against well-established foreign competition made sense to the emerging manufac-turing class. At the same time, southern agriculturalists redefined their ver-sion of political economy, as their section grew increasingly wedded to cash crop agriculture built on the labor of slaves. The tariff became a bitterly divi-sive issue within Congress as each section of the Union sought to reap advan-tages based on its own economic realities.

The American people and their policy makers had an important decision to make about the future of their nation's budding industrial sector: Could American manufacturing, and the agriculturalists that supplied it with raw materials, survive and thrive in a free-trade economic system, or did it require protection? British efforts to flood the American market with cheap imports in the aftermath of the War of 1812, as well as the economic discomfort of 1819–1821 suggested the former. Other considerations, however, placed into question the usefulness and benefit of a tariff. For example, imposing tariffs to protect underdeveloped American industries such as iron and woolen manufacturing might sap the will of manufacturers to invest in maturing their industries. A protective tariff, then, could actually hamper the development of modern manufacturing in the nation. In spite of the perils, by 1824 calls for imposing tariffs had led many influential politicians, like Henry Clay of Kentucky, to develop protectionist legislation.

Clay's American System, with its triune agenda of internal improvements, national banking, and a protective tariff, had emerged as the nationalists' favored means of national economic development. The system's proponents saw the tariff, however, as the key to the success of the system; without protection for home industries, an integrated and nationalized economy could not thrive amid the pressures of international competition. To protectionists, the United States remained a vassal of Great Britain and her domination of Atlantic trade. "The truth is," Clay remarked, "that we are . . . independent colonies of England—politically free, commercially slaves."[30] Britain protected certain elements of its own manufacturing and agricultural sectors while expecting the rest of the world to practice free-trade policies that benefited the British capitalists. Whereas some cautioned that protectionism would stunt the growth of American manufacturing because its favor would prevent capitalists from engaging in healthy competition, Clay and his followers believed the American System, especially the tariff, would produce long-term economic growth by easing infant American manufacturing into the merciless world of free trade and laissez-faire commerce.

At the same time that the tariff, as part of the American System, would provide the scaffolding necessary for building a robust American manufacturing sector, Clay's plan envisioned a means by which manufacturing and commerce would unite the disparate sections of the nation. To his mind, each section of the country would concentrate on producing what it could do best. The South would grow the cotton that would feed northern textile mills, the West would produce the food to feed the urbanizing Northeast, and the Northeast would produce the finished products that the whole nation consumed. The strategy made sense, though Clay and his supporters seemed not to recognize that someday a southerner or westerner could make the same argument about economic vassalage against the Northeast as Clay did against Great Britain.

Some regionalists held out, if only for a short time. Massachusetts's own Daniel Webster delivered a ringing defense of free trade in April 1824, in a speech that Robert Y. Hayne would recall in the Webster-Hayne Debate as "a beautiful and enduring monument" to free trade against the "errors and delusion" of protectionism.[31] Whereas Clay had argued that a tariff schedule would alleviate the economic suffering of three years earlier, Webster retorted that America's unstable financial system, and not the absence of protectionism, had caused the economic depression. Perhaps with memories of the Jeffersonian era embargoes in his mind, Webster endorsed the free market as the only means by American industries such as textile manufacturing could thrive. Perhaps, too, the burgeoning New England economy influenced the congressman's reluctance to support protectionism. The section's recovery from the economic depression far outpaced that of the still-struggling Middle West, which supported the tariff policies introduced in Congress. Boston importers had regained their footing and enjoyed a lucrative free trade with Great Britain and other European nations by 1824.

Webster spoke, however, as northeastern firms transitioned from imports to domestic manufacturing. Eastern investors increasingly placed their capital in the hands of manufacturing rather than import commerce and land speculation, resulting in a greater economic boom in the Northeast. Industry had commenced its transformation of New England and its residents. In the woolens industry alone, New England capitalists from Boston's State Street and beyond had invested $50 million. Admittedly, Congressman Webster himself had supported modest protection schedules in what became the Tariff of 1824, though he maintained a certain element of his free-trade proclivities. By 1828, the newly elected senator recanted his brilliant defense of free trade delivered just four years earlier and lent his support on the Senate floor to a broadly protectionist agenda. In doing so, he merely followed his senatorial constituency as well as the Massachusetts capitalists who had experienced their own conversion upon the arrival of the manufacturing revolution.

Whereas New England embraced manufacturing and demanded a protective tariff to shepherd industry through its infancy, other regions objected to a tax structure that promoted the interests of one section over another. Southerners especially rejected protectionism because, they argued, it would cost them on the imports they purchased and the exports they sold to Great Britain and greater Europe. By 1828, several key southern politicians, mostly from

South Carolina, had articulated elaborate arguments and strong objections against tariffs. At the lead of the South Carolina movement stood John C. Calhoun, erstwhile nationalist and presumptive vice presidential candidate in that year's election for the presidency. Calhoun's ideas represented a significant shift in his own political beliefs, ideas that would resonate throughout the country and provoke a constitutional crisis in the coming years.

2

The South's March toward Sectionalism

"SIR, YOU MAY RAISE THIS ARMY, you may build up this vast structure of patronage, this mighty apparatus of favoritism; but—'lay not the flat-
tering unction to your own souls'—you will never live to enjoy the succes-
sion. You sign your political death warrant."[1] So spoke Virginia's eccentric
congressman John Randolph of Roanoke, who deplored the notion of going to
war against Great Britain. He believed that the War Hawks' belligerent tone
toward the old mother country imperiled the young and defenseless nation—
all for political gain. A December 1811 report from the House Committee on
Foreign Relations confirmed in Randolph's mind that the War Hawks had no
idea what war with Great Britain would entail. On December 11, the tempera-
mental representative delivered a searing condemnation of the case for war
in the House of Representatives in which he predicted the political downfall
of the War Hawks. Though shrill in voice and rhetoric, the "Damned Ras-
cal," as President James Madison called him, marshaled compelling evidence
that the United States was ill prepared to fight a war against one of the most
powerful nations in the world.[2] The regular army numbered four thousand
men, most posted on the western frontier to protect the influx of settlers
from attack by Native Americans. After a decade of neglect, the navy could
not possibly defend the American coastline against the largest maritime force

in the world. To reinforce his claims among southerners, Randolph raised the dreaded possibility that war could provoke a slave revolt. Would northerners infiltrate the South, spreading word of the French Revolution and its calls for equality? And why should the United States ally with France anyway, especially after Napoleon and his regime had violated American sovereignty as well? The Old Republican from Virginia had mounted a compelling and caustic indictment of the War Hawks and their exuberance for a war to assert American nationalism.

The newly elected congressman John C. Calhoun of South Carolina's Abbeville district, himself one of the War Hawks, had already sparred with Virginia's Randolph over the issue of war. Calhoun's star rose quickly in the Twelfth Congress, after Henry Clay awarded him the second rank in the Committee on Foreign Relations. Randolph, who also served on the committee, held the young leaders of the new Congress in contempt. Calhoun and Clay, he remarked to an associate, "have entered this House with their eye on the Presidency, and mark my words sir, we shall have war before the end of the session."[3] Calhoun, showing a "haughty assumption of equality with the oldest and most experienced members of the Congress," made clear that he would show no deference to his elder colleagues.[4]

After Randolph's characteristically vitriolic speech in mid-December, Calhoun decided to refute his colleague's assertions in what would be his first major address in the House. The South Carolinian defended the call for war with a point-by-point rebuttal of Randolph's claims. The Virginian argued that the nation could not mount an offensive against Great Britain, Calhoun noted. What had Randolph done to secure his nation's military? Randolph, Calhoun argued, had "seen the defenceless state of his country . . . under his own eyes, without a single endeavor to remedy so serious an evil."[5] A country with the population and resource potential that the United States possessed could wage war against Great Britain, if only the Congress would mandate preparedness. As for the possibility of slave rebellion, Calhoun dismissed Randolph's claims as fearmongering. Likewise, he rejected Randolph's claims that the southern and western states favored war because of falling cotton and hemp prices. The South sought no war of aggression but did not fear fighting a war of defense. If Randolph wanted peace, Calhoun stated, "let his eloquence be addressed to Lord Wellesley or Mr. Percival, and not the American Congress."[6]

Calhoun's first major speech in Congress won plaudits from his colleagues

Vice President John C. Calhoun, about 1830. The severe South Carolinian served as a mentor to Robert Y. Hayne and may have passed talking points from his perch above the Senate down to Hayne on the floor. Courtesy of the Library of Congress. Reproduction number LC-DIG-ppmsca-19251

and the press. Thomas Ritchie, influential editor of the *Richmond Enquirer*, wrote in his paper that Calhoun would become "one of the master-spirits, who stamp their names upon the age in which they live."[7] Yet the ardent young nationalist from Abbeville could not answer one of Randolph's most important points: Would New England, whose economy depended on maritime commerce with Great Britain, support a war that threatened its livelihood? Randolph predicted trouble ahead with New England. Calhoun's speech exuded the notion that all Americans, whether in the South, West, or New England, would unite behind the common defense of the country against a foreign enemy. Calhoun the nationalist could not fathom any other possibility. Of course, the war would prove his optimism wrong. The war's aftermath, however, would give Calhoun and his fellow southern leaders the opportunity to chart a path toward new nationalism, even if it only lasted for a decade.

After three years of war, James Madison could finally pivot to domestic concerns. In his penultimate annual message to Congress, the Virginia president sketched a program of national development that delighted some and worried others as it pointed toward the Era of Good Feelings over which his successor would preside. Northerners expressed differing opinions on the program of national development that the president revealed, but Madison had to pay careful attention to dissent in his own backyard. Southern nationalists like Calhoun and Clay delighted at the message, but the Virginia Old Republicans believed that their president had surrendered to the nationalizing principles of Federalism. In a critique of the Madison agenda, the always belligerent Randolph stated that the message "out-Hamilton's Alexander Hamilton," referring to the nation's first secretary of the treasury, who had forcefully advocated economic nationalism for the fledgling nation.[8] Times had changed, however; the opponents of Federalism in the 1790s, including Madison himself, feared that the nationalizing program would serve the moneyed interests and the Anglophiles rather than the people. Nearly twenty years later, the president had seen how the positive elements of nationalism had led to growth and prosperity. He also saw where hostility to national development had hindered American progress. Now that Americans had once again thrown off British aggression, now that the nation began to see its potential as a commercial and agricultural state, Madison proposed, in the words of his biographer, "to let a free people *use* their representative government to fulfill national objectives."[9]

Congress, with the War Hawk nationalists still in place, agreed with the president's outlook and took steps to implement it rapidly. Many of Madison's Virginian friends, however, opposed the new program. A decade of economic decline had left the Virginia agricultural economy in a perilous position. Poor yields and uncertain prices left farmers and planters searching for solutions. Some moved west seeking more fertile lands, a development that mirrored the population exodus that New Englanders likewise lamented. Decreasing population led to diminishing political influence, as the Old Dominion fell behind New York and Pennsylvania in congressional representation. Land prices in the East plummeted amid the western land rush. Through it all, the Virginia Dynasty lost considerable influence and allure both during and after the War of 1812, leaving many Virginians searching for an explanation. Many saw the postwar nationalist agenda as the reason why the decline of Virginia continued—and why it might accelerate in the future.

The Old Republicans felt marginalized in the postwar period as localism gave way to nationalism. Men like John Taylor of Caroline saw tyranny looming in the details of the nationalist agenda. Taylor and his associates argued that the manufacturing and commercial interests, aided by preferential government policy, would overshadow the agrarian majority. This Adam Smith disciple saw an insidious visible hand—the federal government—plucking wealth from the pockets of farmers only to deposit it in the hands of manufacturers. Faced with an economic and political onslaught that threatened their preeminence, Virginians looked to states' rights and strict construction of the Constitution as their defense against changes they could not control otherwise. With the federal government acting as an agent of change and development contrary to the interests of Virginia, the Old Dominion's leaders sought to wrest control away from Washington and place it in Richmond.

While southerners in Virginia and North Carolina fretted about their future role in the Union, the stream of emigrants headed to the South and West sought to capitalize on postwar prosperity. Agriculture, not manufacturing and commerce, fueled the boom between 1815 and 1819 in the Southwest. Three economic factors undergirded the boom cycle: easy credit, plentiful federal lands for sale, and strong demand for southern agricultural exports in Europe. Southwestern farmers had purchased land on credit in record numbers. The federal government had $22,000,000 in land debt on its books, due in full on September 30, 1819, half of which came from land purchases in Alabama and Mississippi, where a cotton belt was developing along the fertile interior river valleys.[10] Reliable statistics for state bank debt do not exist, but most historians agree that farmers owed even more to the wildcat banks, as some observers called them in the aftermath of the coming economic collapse, that granted loans liberally in the second half of the 1810s.

Who were the farmers borrowing massive sums of money to purchase land? As was usual in most land bonanzas in American history, the recipients of credit varied widely. A substantial number of upstart farmers who had moved west to escape exhausted soils and poor crop yields borrowed on credit and a prayer that staple prices would remain high. Land speculators, however, accounted for much of the frenzied borrowing as well. They took advantage of the land-credit system, established in 1800 to promote the sale of western lands to yeomen farmers, to buy low and sell high. Policy makers knew that the system had problems, but they could not agree on a remedy that would balance the desire to check speculation and potential fraud with the Jeffersonian impulse to create an agrarian republic in the West.

By 1818, the storm clouds of economic peril had formed on the horizon. European agriculture began to stabilize with the end of war on the continent. American exports of grains and meat flagged; then cotton prices fell dramatically. Southern agriculturalists, especially in the debt-ridden Southwest, faltered as debt payments exceeded income. Local banks in the South and West, but especially in Kentucky, Alabama, and Tennessee, began to call in loans and contract the paper money supply. These wildcat banks had skirted the rules by maintaining inadequate specie reserves in their vaults. When customers sought to redeem paper money for gold and silver, the banks exhausted their reserves and had to suspend payment in specie.

The wildcat banks, in many respects, received encouragement from the Second Bank of the United States. Established in 1817 to regulate the issuance of state bank notes and to stabilize the nation's monetary system, the bank had almost the opposite effect in the South and West because of profligate leadership. People in the new states and territories welcomed the bank with a curious blend of support and opposition. Prospective borrowers desperate for credit welcomed the national bank, but some southerners with states' rights predilections opposed its creation as an unconstitutional extension of federal authority. State banks, sensing competition and fearing the bank's mandate to regulate paper money, likewise opposed the institution. The bank's directors sought to curry favor with the hostile southerners and westerners by indirectly supporting the state banks with much-needed capital and by issuing loans freely, contrary to the purported wishes of Congress and the treasury. By 1818, the problems inherent in the bank's policy of loose credit became all too apparent. The directors restricted the redemption of paper notes and began to collect on overdue balances from southern and western branches as well as the wildcat banks.

Southern banks proved especially vulnerable to the economic disaster, as they generally possessed lower specie reserves than did their northern counterparts. Southern and western overextension had a cascading effect on the rest of the nation as well. Any one branch of the bank was obligated to redeem the notes of other branches. By 1818, the New England branches of the Bank of the United States had expended significant specie reserves in redeeming notes from southern and western branches that had exhausted their own reserves.[11] The quickening pace of contraction, designed to stop the drain of specie reserves that had dwindled, began to wreak havoc on the southwestern economy.

A second crisis emerged as the country began to feel the effects of the Panic of 1819. Thomas Jefferson likened it to a "fire bell in the night" that threatened the Union itself.[12] Like the panic, the crisis started in the West and spread east to the halls of power in Washington. The admission of Missouri to the Union sparked a discussion over slavery and the power of the federal government that changed the way that southerners looked at the nation and its constituent states. It hearkened a southern retreat from postwar nationalism and inaugurated a new era of states' rights politics that would come to define southern beliefs about *"imperium in imperio"*—a state within a state.

Representative James Tallmadge Jr. of New York opposed the extension of slavery into Missouri for several reasons. First, Tallmadge genuinely opposed the institution of slavery at a time when his home state neared the end of its process of emancipation. And though New York and the other northern states had ended slavery within their borders, the institution had burgeoned in the South, especially in the southwestern states where planters developed the cotton belt. Second, Tallmadge and his northern Republican colleagues feared the outsized political power that southerners had gained with the 30 percent expansion of slavery during the 1810s. The three-fifths compromise in the Constitution apportioned representation based on the free white population as well as three-fifths of the slave population. The ever-increasing slave population in the South added to the section's political power, according to a number of northern Republicans who feared the excessive southern domination of national politics.

When Tallmadge rose in the House of Representatives on February 13, 1819, to introduce an amendment to the Missouri statehood bill prohibiting "the further introduction of slavery or involuntary servitude" and providing for the eventual manumission of slaves within its borders, he set into motion a furious debate that roused the South to defend its peculiar institution and its political power, which some leaders believed was already imperiled by economic distress and other ominous developments within the national government.[13] After the initial shock and the opening volley in the war of words that spanned two congresses, it became clear that the debate over statehood for Missouri had inaugurated a new phase in the discussion over the extension of slavery, its effect on American politics, and the idea of slavery itself. Southern politics changed after the Missouri debates, as southerners realized that antislavery Americans could use the politics of territory making and statehood formation as a means of confining slavery to where it currently existed—or even abolish it at some future date.

For as many southerners alarmed by the fire bell in the night ringing from the floors of the House and Senate, still others saw a similar threat coming from one floor below in the Capitol building. In its crypt-like basement quarters, John Marshall's US Supreme Court had been hard at work on its own nationalist agenda. The chief justice, a John Adams appointee, had attempted over the course of his eighteen-year tenure to make the judiciary a coequal branch of government. The Virginian, no friend of the likes of Randolph and Taylor, also sought to imbue American law with two cherished Federalist principles: federal supremacy over the states and the primacy of the Supreme Court to interpret the law. *Marbury v. Madison* (1803) asserted the latter, but Marshall deemed the former principle a work in progress. By 1819, however, the Marshall court had developed a body of case law that left states' rights advocates dismayed and fearful for their own principle of state supremacy within the Union. Then the court handed down its decision in *McCulloch v. Maryland* on March 6, 1819, just three days after Congress had adjourned from its tempestuous session in which James Tallmadge had sought to encumber slavery in the prospective state of Missouri.

The McCulloch case had nothing to do with slavery, but it addressed other concerns that animated westerners and southerners. The State of Maryland had sought to impose a tax on the Baltimore branch of the Bank of the United States because its legislators viewed the national bank as a threat to smaller state-chartered banks operating within the state. Five other states had attempted the same policy; two states banned the institution outright. James W. McCulloch, the cashier of the Baltimore branch, refused to pay the tax, and a lawsuit ensued. Lower courts upheld Maryland's right to tax the bank, but the case ended up before the Supreme Court on appeal, where two fundamental questions surfaced as a result of the litigation. Did states have the right to regulate a creation of Congress? More fundamentally, did Congress have the right to create a bank?

Circumstances surrounding the bank further complicated matters. In the wake of the ensuing Panic of 1819, the Bank of the United States had few friends because of its directors' maladministration of affairs prior to the economic collapse and its feeble management thereafter. Many Americans blamed the bank for failing to use its power to regulate the supply of paper money issued by state-chartered banks, which had fueled the economic boom. The bank had ridden the heights of the boom alongside the wildcat banks, and then when the collapse began, it changed course rapidly, leaving smaller banks and debtors facing ruin. Investigations had also revealed fraud and corruption within the bank and its branches. Indeed, McCulloch himself had engaged in massive fraud at the Baltimore branch, issuing $3 million in paper notes that its directors knew it could not redeem in specie and that other branches would have to honor contractually. McCulloch himself reaped a $500,000 windfall in loans made with no collateral; the malevolent Baltimore cashier owned no property.

Against this backdrop of deception, a unanimous Supreme Court issued its ruling in *McCulloch v. Maryland*. Writing for a unanimous court, Marshall addressed first the question of whether Congress had the authority to create a national bank. The court argued that it indeed did possess the implied power under the necessary and proper clause of the Constitution. True, Congress had created the bank as a private entity, but it served a public purpose and therefore functioned as an arm of the federal government. Because the bank had a public purpose as a regulator of the monetary system, the states could not tax the institution. Marshall's now-famous line that "the power to tax involves the power to destroy" created a wall of protection around the bank's operations that no state could violate without impeding the legitimate operation of the federal government's constitutional authority to collect taxes, borrow money, and regulate commerce.[14]

Southerners and westerners alike had attacked the bank with the onset of the panic, but after the *McCulloch* decision they likewise assailed the court. *Richmond Enquirer* editor Thomas Ritchie saw *McCulloch v. Maryland* as the culmination of a series of "alarming errors of the Supreme Court of the United States in their interpretation of the Constitution."[15] Saving a bank that had violated, and in some instances abused, its authority raised concerns, but Ritchie and many southerners believed the case was "fraught with alarming consequences" beyond economics.[16] In upholding congressional authority to create the bank, the court had given greater legitimacy to the principle of broad constitutional construction. One Virginia observer lamented that the court could apply the same principle to the "seductive system of internal improvements, and national grandeur" that nationalists advocated.[17] Others worried about a far greater danger: federal authority over slavery.

A subtle but powerful shift in public opinion emerged in the South and West after 1819, as the Old Republicans of Virginia began to convince their fellow citizens that abstract constitutional principles like strict versus broad construction possessed real importance to the citizenry. The bank had exacerbated if not caused economic ruin south of the Mason-Dixon Line. It had failed to stem the collapse of agricultural prices that continued for two years after the Panic of 1819 commenced. Cotton had fallen by over 50 percent; tobacco prices had plummeted by 90 percent. Other matters beyond economic concerns alarmed southerners in particular. James Tallmadge's amendment to prohibit slavery in Missouri as a condition of statehood seemed unprecedented to southerners, who increasingly saw slavery as the cornerstone of their livelihood and their way of life. Slaveholders wondered if broad construction of the Constitution could lead to congressional authority over their peculiar institution—slavery. Congress had adjourned without settling the issue, but the vitriolic debate over Missouri statehood had imperiled the Jeffersonian alliance of northern and southern Republicans. Northern public opinion supported the Tallmadge amendment, while southerners looked aghast at the merging threat to westward expansion in the Mississippi River valley and to the peculiar institution itself. For a growing number of white southerners, abstract principles had suddenly become more concrete.

Amid the constitutional tumult over *McCulloch* and the economic turmoil wrought by the panic, the Missouri crisis resumed with the next session of Congress. President James Monroe summoned the members of his cabinet to the Executive Mansion on March 3, 1820, to discuss a matter of utmost urgency: after a year of bruising debate in Congress and in the court of public opinion, Congress had crafted legislation that promised to settle the dispute over slavery and Missouri statehood. The District of Maine, long a part of Massachusetts, would become a free state, while Missouri would join the Union as a slave state. That left the issue of slavery in the remainder of the Louisiana Purchase an unsettled question. To address the issue and restore harmony to a divided Congress, Senator Jesse B. Thomas of Illinois proposed drawing a line between free and slave territory at 36° 30' north latitude. The legislation prohibited slavery north of the line and permitted it to the south. Dividing territory between freedom and slavery was hardly a new idea in the history of slavery's extension to the West. The president, however, could not decide for himself whether Thomas's provision was constitutional. Therefore, he asked the cabinet members to state their opinion, in writing, on two issues. First, did Congress have the right to prohibit slavery in a territory? Second, did the slavery prohibition in the bill pertain only to a territory or did its force extend into statehood? On the latter question, the cabinet found consensus only after Monroe reworded his query (and hedged on its meaning) to ask whether the interdiction was compatible with the Constitution. On the former question, all agreed that Congress could indeed prohibit slavery in a territory. Secretary of War John C. Calhoun conceded that the Constitution gave Congress "no express authority" to regulate slavery but that the implied powers clause probably sufficed for authority.[18] Satisfied with the responses submitted by his cabinet, Monroe signed the legislation into law on March 6.[19]

After the meeting on March 3, Calhoun and Secretary of State John Quincy Adams walked home together from the Executive Mansion and continued their discussion of the slavery issue. Adams had taken an antislavery position during the meeting on the grounds that slavery violated the natural rights of man. In their conversation Calhoun expressed his respect for Adams's opinions on the rights of man, but he argued that most southerners believed those rights extended only to white men. Calhoun attempted to explain the complicated race relations between whites and enslaved African Americans in the South, a system in which slaves engaged in domestic labor, while whites managed the operations of vast agricultural enterprises. Adams could not understand Calhoun's description; to the Massachusetts native's mind, linking slavery with labor degraded the very idea of a person earning a living by hard work. Calhoun sought to address Adams's objections by distinguishing between ordinary manual labor and farming, a vocation that some southern whites engaged in without the aid of slaves. Calhoun drew from an ambiguity in the labor theory of value that allowed slaveholders to appropriate an enslaved person's labor as their own. Since an enslaved person was property, a slaveholder could claim ownership of his or her labor. At the same time, slaveholders like Calhoun claimed that their status as free people gave them ownership of their labor and the land they used to make their living.[20]

The secretary of state confided to his diary that he could not accept Calhoun's tortured logic on the matter. Indeed, Adams discerned a contradiction in Calhoun's beliefs: the South Carolinian defended slavery even as he apologized for it. In actuality, during the Missouri debates both men had encountered an important facet of the argument between the supporters and opponents of slavery. The Missouri controversy had laid bare a moral debate that intensified over the coming forty years. Southerners became alarmed at the moral outrage against slavery that surfaced in the debates of 1819 and 1820. Before Missouri, they had viewed slavery as a necessary evil; after 1820, southerners inched toward a defense of slavery as a positive good and as a sacrosanct institution within southern borders. The movement within Congress to halt the extension of slavery caused further concern when placed within the context of an economic depression caused by a national bank and the pronouncements of a Supreme Court that shifted the balance of power between the national government and the states toward the former. The southern retreat toward a defensive position had commenced.

George McDuffie, a congressman from South Carolina, offers one of the most vivid—even extreme—examples of how southern nationalists transformed from economic nationalism to political sectionalism. Alas, McDuffie was a man of extremes. The orphaned child of poor Scottish immigrants to Georgia, young McDuffie exhibited the traits of brilliance as well as intemperance in his speech. Elected to Congress in 1820, McDuffie distinguished himself as a proponent of the economic nationalism that his fellow South Carolinian John C. Calhoun espoused and an enemy of the states' rights creed of the Old Republicans of Virginia and North Carolina. Working within the fractured politics of the early 1820s—the Era of Good Feelings had become history—McDuffie attacked states' rights as the "climax of political heresies."[21] In a letter to supporters of William H. Crawford, a Georgia politician, states' rights advocate, and presidential aspirant, McDuffie spurned the tenets of localism that had begun to creep into southern politics since 1819. The Constitution, wrote McDuffie in 1821, "was formed by the people, and for the people," and not, he implied, by the states. The Union served the people's will. "Popular in its creation and its objects, *it was intended that it should be construed by the plain and obvious dictates of common sense, and with a liberal regard to the great national ends it was designed to accomplish.*"[22] McDuffie anticipated the idea that a state could attempt to nullify federal law, a development he denounced in no uncertain terms. A state refusing to enforce a revenue law, for example, "would be the very case which the [constitutional] convention had in view, when they made provisions for 'calling forth the militia to enforce the laws of the Union.'" To McDuffie's mind, a dual sovereignty could not exist; "in all governments there must be some *one* supreme power."[23]

Unfortunately for McDuffie, his brief in favor of economic nationalism also included a characteristically vituperative assault on his opponents. One of the offended Crawfordites demanded satisfaction on the field of honor. McDuffie, an inexperienced duelist, suffered a dreadful spinal wound that slowly paralyzed him and finally killed him some thirty years later. The Calhounites cried foul and charged the Crawford supporters, incorrectly, with attempting political assassination against the nationalist McDuffie. But the essay, as well as the ensuing duel over its contents, revealed the extreme changes sweeping over southern politics. Factionalism had all but destroyed the Jeffersonian Republican coalition, leaving party unity a distant dream. The loss of unity came at a time when southerners feared, perhaps more than ever, for the economic and political preeminence of their region. The people that McDuffie wrote of in his essay drifted away from economic nationalism and toward political sectionalism, leaving the nationalists in a quandary. And again, McDuffie offers the most extreme example of how they responded: the ardent nationalist of 1821 who had fought a duel to defend his beliefs in national supremacy became one of the most zealous proponents of sectionalism and even nullification within six short years.

Mighty forces worked against economic nationalism in the South during the 1820s, but the position against national development developed slowly. Countervailing forces made the politics of improvement difficult. On the one hand, southerners emerged from the panic and the Missouri debates with a renewed apprehension about the exercise of federal power. On the other hand, entire regions of the South found the idea of national development appealing because it promised better connections between market centers and hinterlands. The debate between nationalism and localism bore a significant part of the discussion over internal improvements, pitting the middle and southern Atlantic states against the emerging West. The General Survey Act of 1824, legislation authorizing surveying for roads and canals throughout the nation, illustrated the differences. In the House of Representatives, congressmen from the nine western states—three free and six slave—voted unanimously for the bill. By a margin of fifteen to thirty-four, the south Atlantic congressmen voted against the bill.[24] The Atlantic states tended to oppose the bill because they had already constructed roads and canals, but in

Virginia and the Carolinas, the Old Republicans had railed against a national improvement policy because it violated the principles of strict construction and threatened to abet those who sought the expansion of federal power.

That the American people would elect a new president in 1824 also loomed over the situation. The disintegration of the Jeffersonian Republican Party and the emergence of factional politics based more on regional loyalties and personal popularity boded ill for coordinated national development. After John Quincy Adams's election to the presidency, the southern factions coalesced into parties for and against the new president. Andrew Jackson in particular played off the southern fears of a Federalist revival under the new chief executive. Opponents of the administration tended toward a platform that called for greater democracy and adherence to states' rights. Internal improvements faced an uncertain future within the realigned political order, but an even greater issue emerged that southerners latched onto as a threat to their section and their way of life.

During the 1820s, the protective tariff emerged as the preeminent economic issue in American politics. Congressional debates over tariff policy in 1820 and 1824 revealed differences between the manufacturing Northeast and the agricultural South and West. Overemphasizing stark sectional differences, however, obscures more specific regional concerns. Kentucky, with its connections to the Ohio River trade, sided with the Northwest in favor of both internal improvements and a protective tariff. Markets for Kentucky hemp improved with the Northeast's business fortunes. In regions without substantial connections to northeastern mercantile interests, however, opposition ran deep. Northern economic nationalists endorsed a protective tariff as the best means to ensure the growth of American manufacturing, but southerners—even nationalists like Calhoun—opposed even the mildest protectionism. For southern nationalists, the problem with a protective tariff hinged on the definition of general welfare. Tariffs provided aid to some at the cost of others. Much in the way that they opposed federal funding for local internal improvement projects, southern nationalists believed that federal policy must benefit the entire Union and not merely one constituency.

Southerners saw two problems with the economics of a protective tariff, both serious enough to provoke vigorous opposition. First, tariffs protected industries that would not otherwise survive in a free market, thereby increasing costs for consumers and favoring products inferior to those produced in more mature industrial economies. The textiles of New England, for example, could not compare in either cost or quality to those of Great Britain. To a section of planters accustomed to international trade and finance, buying American seemed illogical when one could obtain a better product at a cheaper price elsewhere. Moreover, tariffs restrained the invisible hand by encouraging investment in less viable opportunities. Supporting inefficient industry, therefore, slowed economic growth. Second, tariffs provoked trade wars between nations, and given its economic system, the South could not win in such a contest. Southern planters sold little of their crops in the United States; instead, they relied on foreign markets. The tariff could not provide them an economic benefit, and it could cause them a great deal of harm. When countries like Great Britain made the inevitable decision to place tariffs on American exports in retaliation for American duties on foreign imports, the South would suffer disproportionately. Demand for staple crops such as cotton and rice would decrease as foreign nations found alternative sources. In sum, southern planters believed that tariffs would increase costs for the goods they purchased abroad and stifle demand for their exports.

A poor economy heightened southern concerns about the ill effects of protective tariffs. Southern agriculture languished even after much of the country had recovered from the Panic of 1819. At the same time, northeastern manufacturing rebounded and even expanded. Both sections underwent a prolonged and oftentimes painful economic realignment after the panic, but the South faced straitened conditions longer than the North did. As the northeasterners rushed into their emerging manufacturing economy, they called for protection of their infant industries. Meanwhile, southern agriculture looked to continued free trade as its saving grace. When Congress debated a revised tariff schedule in 1820, southern representatives insisted that free trade, not protectionism, would produce economic growth. Virginia representative John Tyler, who twenty years later would become president, conceded that the tariff would produce a short-term economic boost as protectionism made investment in manufacturing more attractive. The results would be fleeting, however, as workers demanded higher wages, costs increased, and American manufacturing would once again face challenges from cheaper European competition. The cycle, Tyler argued, would continually repeat itself. Conspicuous in Tyler's argument, and in those of his southern colleagues, was the Jeffersonian notion that wage labor would create, in the words of another Virginia representative, "a population distorted and decrepid [sic], as respects both bodily and mental endowments, especially marked by imbecility and abasement." He exclaimed, "How unlike our ances-tors achieving the Revolution."[25]

Political changes made matters seem more urgent as well. The southern congressional delegation narrowly defeated tariff increases in 1820, but four years later reapportionment changed representation in Congress, diminish-ing southern power and making its politicians more protective of their region and its interests. Debate over the tariff of 1824 shifted in favor of enhanced protection, a political and economic development that worried southerners. After the census of 1820, westward migration had changed the demographics of the nation. The free states were outpacing the slave states in westward ex-pansion, which showed in the reapportioned House of Representatives. The northern states gained twenty seats in the House, while the South added only eleven.

Southern politicians debating in the 1820 deliberations over tariff policy developed a comprehensive case against protectionism, but they did not de-clare tariffs unconstitutional. The omission bears significance given how of-ten early American politicians debated constitutional interpretation. Internal improvements had provoked a discussion of strict versus broad construction, wherein southerners disagreed over the elasticity of their founding charter, but the southern position on the tariff remained undeveloped. By 1824, how-ever, the lines of contention had started to change and some southerners began to question whether the federal government could or should use its power to levy tariffs to achieve a change in economic policy. Strict construc-tionists began to develop the argument that the federal government could use a tariff to raise revenue for operations but could not do so to aid a particular industry. A revenue tariff, they argued, taxed from necessity; a tariff for pro-tection made the federal government the agent of privileged economic inter-ests. Again, they founded their opposition on the belief that tariffs arbitrarily picked winners and losers within the economy. Senator Robert Y. Hayne of South Carolina decried the inherent favoritism of the tariff policy, threaten-ing that "if capitalists will, in the face of our protests and in defiance of our solemn warnings, invest their fortunes in pursuits made profitable at our ex-pense, on their own heads be the consequences of their folly."[26]

The increasingly heated rhetoric among southern hotspurs in Congress came as southern nationalists, especially in South Carolina, faced pressure to reconsider their support for internal improvements, national banking, and protective tariffs. The nationalist program, which hewed closely to the principles of Henry Clay's American System, faltered amid competing sectional plans, even as a president committed to an expansive vision of national power waited to replace the last of the Virginia Dynasty. Across New York, then down the Ohio River valley and west to Missouri, where rivers and canals had integrated the rural population with the eastern manufacturing and mercantile economy, support for economic nationalism remained strong. Some New Englanders remained ambivalent about the program, but their opposition eroded as their economy evolved toward manufacturing. In the South, however, most agriculturalists opposed the tariff and saw internal improvements beyond their immediate region as a misappropriation of taxpayer dollars.

For southern nationalists like John C. Calhoun, the political future of nationalism seemed bleak. The Tariff of 1824 increased duties on cotton and wool by a third. Cotton was beginning to ascend its throne as king of the southern staple crops; wool clothed the enslaved people who planted, tended, and harvested the cotton. Five years of economic malaise and increasing land taxes strengthened opposition to any measure that would further burden the planter class. The vote on the Tariff of 1824 revealed the emerging sectional differences over protection and, in some way, made southern fears of economic favoritism a self-fulfilling prophecy. The new tariff schedule bore the marks of a policy designed to placate different regions and interests over others, a political strategy that would not disappear in the future. Nor would southern opposition diminish. The economics of national development worried southerners, but so too did other developments that transcended dollars and cents and brought fears of an existential threat to the southern slaveholding oligarchy.

Denmark Vesey of Charleston, South Carolina, stood out among the African American population of his city for at least two reasons: he was literate and he was free. A carpenter and a preacher at the second-largest African Methodist Episcopal church in the United States, Vesey occupied a remarkable place within Charleston society. But in the summer of 1822, Vesey engaged himself in other work that would terrorize white Charlestonians and change race relations within the city thereafter. Vesey had completed plans for a rebellion of the slave and free black community in Charleston to capture the city and perhaps sail to Haiti. Though Vesey had purchased his freedom after winning a lottery, many of his family members remained in bondage. And so the carpenter and preacher began to enlist the support of free and enslaved black artisans in Charleston to capture the city arsenal and control the city. Vesey's plan fell apart, however, when several slaves revealed the plans to their masters. At first the masters seemed incredulous at such wild rumors, but then they began to believe the accounts they heard, and the local militia acted to suppress the rebellion. Authorities executed thirty-five conspirators, including Vesey, and banished thirty-seven more from the United States.

Vesey's plans further alarmed Charlestonians when they learned where he had received the inspiration for the revolt. The preacher had found justification for his plans in the Bible and in the antislavery speeches delivered by northern congressmen during the debate over Missouri statehood. Incensed southerners blamed northern lawmakers and antislavery agitators for interfering in the local affairs of southern communities and for inciting rebellion with outside pamphlets and publications. Clearly, southern slaveholders believed they had much work to do at home in order to safeguard their communities, but they also sought to ban interference with slavery from outside the southern slaveholding regime. To an emerging cadre of southern states' rights politicians, southerners had to find protection against antislavery influences. To Robert Y. Hayne, who once called the Constitution "the very 'Ark of the Covenant,' in which alone we will find safety," circumstances required a strict construction of the nation's founding charter that would prevent Congress from touching any part of the South's peculiar institution.[27]

The debates over slavery and economic policy shared a common thread that bound them together in the minds of many southerners: the necessity of states' rights and strict construction to insulate and protect the South from outside agents of change that threatened its social, political, and economic order. The Old Republicans of Virginia and the planter gentry of South Carolina offer unmistakable evidence of foreboding southern politicians espousing states' rights and strict construction that led to the growing sectionalism that threatened the Union in the future. Virginia and especially South Carolina, however, present the most extreme examples of southern sectionalism during the 1820s. Viewing the South as a monolith distorts the diversity of opinion on key issues that surfaced during the 1820s, especially economics. In other southern states opposition to national development came more slowly and in piecemeal fashion. The southwestern states, for example, continued to see benefit in internal improvements. Hemp planters in Kentucky and sugar planters in Louisiana supported protection because it helped them economically. Accordingly, regional differences played a major role in how southerners interpreted issues such as the American System and President

John Quincy Adams's vision of union. During the Adams presidency, however, political associations realigned and, in general, southerners began to drift away from nationalism toward the safe haven of sectionalism. Above all, sectionalism and strict construction prevented interference with slavery and the internal affairs of southern states. Sectional consciousness changed the southern outlook on liberty, power, and union, leading the South's political leadership toward a more defensive posture against nationalism and an active federal government.

At the moment when southern opposition to the protective tariff began to strengthen, especially in South Carolina, northeastern manufacturers declared the 1824 duties inadequate to protect American products from cheap foreign imports. New England textile manufacturers continued to face pressure from more established British firms whose looms supplied cheaper fabric to American customers. The 1824 debates had proven that tariff policy could become labyrinthine in the ways some industries benefited and others suffered as a result of protection. New England woolens manufacturers were the aggrieved party in 1827; as they argued, the tariff passed by Congress three years earlier had raised tariffs on raw wool, which eroded their profits. The so-called Woolens Bill, which would have raised wool tariffs to almost 50 percent, failed only after John C. Calhoun, now vice president, cast the tie-breaking vote in the Senate to reject the legislation. A convention in Harrisburg, Pennsylvania, in the summer of 1827, which called for increased duties on an array of manufactured goods as well as some raw materials including sugar and hemp, showed southerners that northeasterners would not quit the fight against free trade. Moreover, the protectionists had attempted to secure western support by promising aid for internal improvements in exchange for supporting increased duties. To the minds of many southern leaders, northeasterners were poised to sweep protection through Congress and forge an alliance with westerners—all at the political and economic expense of the South.

Southerners cried foul against what they saw as a northern onslaught against their section and—make no mistake—they increasingly saw themselves as part of not a mere region but a beleaguered section that was becoming a political minority. Two students of the southern economy, political economist Thomas Cooper and influential planter Robert Turnbull, decried protection and the efforts of those who had met at Harrisburg to thwart free trade and ally with the West. Both blamed the tariff for the South's straitened

economic condition; both accused northern leaders of playing special-inter-
est politics; both resorted to states' rights arguments to combat the northeastern agenda. Cooper famously intoned his solemn warning that southerners
would have "to calculate the value of the Union, and ask of what use to us is
this most unequal alliance."[28]

Few observers had assessed the situation as closely as John C. Calhoun,
who seemed caught between his nationalist proclivities and the increasing
states' rights fervor of his South Carolina contemporaries. Palmetto State
leaders lined up against economic nationalism, which they blamed for the
ruinous economic conditions in the South, but Calhoun's own research found
the planters at least partially liable for their own misfortunes. Cotton planters had exacerbated their precarious condition by increasing production at a
time of declining prices, a problem that had nothing to do with tariff policy.
Supply and demand worked against planters in a market glutted with cotton.
The vice president, however, had come to believe that the tariff bore at least
some responsibility. Politically, he may not have had a choice, as his constituents seemed convinced that protectionism had endangered their economy.
Calhoun found particular fault with the Adams administration itself, which
he believed had used its influence to craft economic policy that benefited the
North over the South. When Calhoun shared his thoughts, some believed that
he had at last abandoned economic nationalism, but he did not see things
that way. To the contrary, he argued, President Adams and Henry Clay had
perverted true nationalism to protect special interests at the expense of the
people. Nationalism had strayed from true principles under the leadership of
a Yankee president and a grasping secretary of state positioning himself as the
administration's second in command.

No southern state felt the sting of economic depression more acutely than
South Carolina. The Panic of 1819 endured in the Palmetto State for reasons
unique to the place itself. Southern agriculturalists all suffered during the
early 1820s, but in states like Virginia, farmers sustained themselves by plant-
ing less tobacco and more mixed crops to feed their families. Neighbors es-
caped the scarcity of money by bartering with one another for what they
needed. Virginians had seen hard times before and had learned hard lessons
that kept them from overextending themselves with easy credit. Cotton planters on the southwestern frontier felt greater pressure from the panic because
so many of them had mortgaged themselves to the limit in order to purchase
land. Fresh lands produced higher yields that helped sustain many frontier

planters in the short term, even if they contributed to excess supply on the international market. South Carolina's problems, however, exceeded those of virtually any other state in the South. Cotton and rice planters in South Carolina had engaged in profligate spending by mortgaging their properties. Too many planters preferred to live in Charleston while overseers managed the plantations, a practice that led to chronic poor management. When trouble struck, be it economic depression, bad harvests, or even hurricanes—as occurred during the early 1820s—destroyed lowland crops, South Carolina planters found themselves ill equipped to weather the turbulence.

South Carolina planters found themselves on the margins at a time when many within their ranks left the state for better opportunities. Between 1820 and 1840, over 132,000 white South Carolinians moved to the southwestern frontier. They took with them an estimated eighty-seven thousand slaves, which amounted to a 40 percent population decline. A demographic decline had hit the state at a time when its leadership class, which had always enjoyed a greater power status than those of other states, felt as if their world was disappearing. South Carolina's planters saw the northeastern manufacturing class as a direct threat to their economic self-sufficiency and political dominance. The planter class developed and espoused a simple—if not entirely correct—theory on how the tariff aggrieved South Carolina. In his "forty bale theory," the nationalist turned states' rights zealot George McDuffie posited that a 40 percent tariff on cloth manufactured from cotton would lead to a domino effect on the market. It would increase the price of cotton cloth by a corresponding percentage, which would lead to a 40 percent drop in cloth sales and finally to a 40 percent cut in planters' income. McDuffie had failed at economics, but he excelled at rhetoric. The tariff—and not exhausted soils, overspending, depopulation, and calamity—had led to ruin in South Carolina.[29]

Few politicians understood the politics of the tariff as did Martin Van Buren of New York. For two years, the Red Fox of Kinderhook, a nickname that referenced Van Buren's hometown as well as his wily political skills, had sought to rebuild the old Jeffersonian coalition with Andrew Jackson as the standard-bearer. Uniting the "planters of the South and the plain Republicans of the North" would, as he explained to the veteran Virginia politico Thomas Ritchie, stymie the ultranationalist Adams agenda, promote democracy for the common man, and squelch the agitation over slavery.[30] In order for Van Buren's plan to succeed, however, he and his operatives had to build a coalition that ensured respect for states' rights while building a cohesive political organization that could compete amid the intense regional loyalties that had dominated American politics for almost a decade. Having secured support for his enterprise from Ritchie, Calhoun, and a number of other leading southern politicians, Van Buren set to work preparing for the 1828 election season.

The tariff, however, complicated matters for Van Buren, the "Little Magician." Northerners demanded protection after the Woolens Bill failed on Calhoun's tiebreaking vote, but southerners, especially in South Carolina, resisted with unprecedented fervor. The nascent Jacksonian coalition could not bring cohesion to the chaotic debate over tariff duties in 1828, and everyone wanted something form the deliberations. A Louisiana senator explained the dizzying array of competing interests: "Maine complains of the Iron & hemp [duties]—New England of the molasses the South of every thing—Penna. insists on the Iron, Ky on the hemp—N. York on the woolens—Penna. agrees to ease Maine on the Molasses—if she will take the Iron. . . . Maine implores & is obstinate—N England sickens with the Molasses & hesitates—The South tell them, it is a Naucious Medium, but will do them good & will work-off the Tariff fever."[31]

Working from the Senate, where he represented New York, the Little Magician had assembled an almost incomprehensible package of duties designed to reward regions supporting Jackson while punishing his opponents. Van Buren saw in the tariff debates what opponents of protection feared: in a political atmosphere ruled by regional loyalties, an enterprising politician could build strong political combinations by manipulating tariff rates. The bill certainly seemed to benefit the "plain Republicans" that Van Buren needed for his northern coalition while assuaging the South as well as possible. Historians have debated the motives of Van Buren and his lieutenants in creating the labyrinthine schedules. Some claim that Van Buren, knowing that the Northeast demanded a tariff bill, created a system so obnoxious to northeastern manufacturers that they would defeat it; others argue that he tried to curry southern support by portraying the legislation as a compromise.[32]

Van Buren conferenced with Calhoun on the bill and presented the vice president with two options. Southerners could join forces with New England manufacturers to defeat the schedules as drafted, but this strategy would lead to an amended bill supported by westerners and easterners, who would take something over nothing. Or southerners could block any effort from New England to raise rates via amendment and hope that they would join forces with the South to defeat a bill that did not accomplish their goals. Vice President Calhoun approved the latter strategy, but it soon backfired when the New England delegation swallowed its pride and accepted the unamended schedules. Congress passed the "Tariff of Abominations" on May 19, 1828, and President Adams signed it into law thereafter. Calhoun and the South howled at the outcome and blasted Van Buren for his connivance. In fact, Van Buren believed he had done the southerners—and himself—a favor by winning votes in moderate tariff states while forestalling even higher duties that would have also cost Jackson the South in his bid for the presidency.[33]

Fierce resistance emerged from the Palmetto State leaders, who called for states' rights and strict construction of the Constitution. The South Carolinians detested the high duties on wool, which they used to clothe slaves. Moreover, they believed that the tariff had become a threat to their rights. Manufactures had once again robbed southern wealth for their own personal benefit, and the federal government had abetted them in the crime. The Adams administration seemed all too eager to further its nationalist agenda at the expense of the southern agricultural states, which struck men like Calhoun as a betrayal of true nationalism. The Supreme Court, with John Marshall as chief justice, had abetted the nationalists through judicial review, a doctrine that Calhoun characterized as "giving to the General Government the sole and final right of interpreting the Constitution—thereby reversing the whole system, making that instrument the creature of its will."[34]

The firebrands in South Carolina demanded action after Adams signed the Tariff of Abominations into law. Meeting in Representative Robert Y. Hayne's boardinghouse quarters, the South Carolina legislative delegation discussed what had happened and how they should respond. George McDuffie, once the ardent nationalist who had inveighed against states' rights as dangerous folly, argued that the tariff would lead to disunion. Most of his colleagues agreed, because by now the tariff issues had transcended economics in the minds of South Carolinians. The tariff debate had revealed a greater threat that the Palmetto State's leaders had to address by protecting individual liberty against an overweening federal government and defending the planters of the South against the industrialists of New England, with whom the president and his lieutenants had sided. Adams supported northern industrialization and seemed to indicate grander designs for national development, leading many southerners to wonder if he had plans to transform the southern economy that might even involve ending slavery. For the moment, moderation prevailed as the delegation agreed to suspend any action until after the presidential election, in which they hoped that Andrew Jackson would become president, with John C. Calhoun as his vice president and the South's behind-the-scenes power broker. Many southerners believed that Jackson, with Calhoun at his side, would support a renegotiation of the tariff schedules.

Vice President Calhoun may have agreed with much of what his colleagues had articulated, but he urged moderation and caution. Calhoun, too, had national political aspirations, which loose talk of redress through disunion could jeopardize. But when Calhoun left the capital for home after the conclusion of the congressional session, he found the mid-Atlantic states in furor over the tariff. He quickly learned that the planters and farmers, especially in South Carolina, believed that the time for restraint had passed. Calhoun the vice president wanted to quiet the shrill rhetoric, but Calhoun the South Carolina politician knew that he had to pay attention to the angry words of his constituents.

On returning home to the South Carolina upcountry, Calhoun received an invitation from William Campbell Preston, an upcountry congressman, to assist the state legislature by writing a report on the tariff and offering ways to seek redress of the state's concerns. Calhoun had to proceed cautiously, however, for the situation was fraught with political consequences. Up to this point in the deliberations over protection, Calhoun had played the role of moderator, seeking to convince his friends that South Carolina meant no ill will toward the Union while attempting to satisfy his constituents that he would stand firm for their rights and grievances. He had to strike the proper tone: to assuage the concerns of his fellow Palmetto State citizens in terms strong enough to garner their support while not jeopardizing his relations with the Jacksonians through intemperate talk of radical ideas. His relationship with the general's associates, however, had already strained political ties. Calhoun disliked Van Buren and blamed him for the tariff, but the New Yorker was fast becoming an important Jackson ally. The emerging party organization that Van Buren labored to make a reality worried Calhoun.

Armed with a trove of sources brought from Washington, Calhoun headed home to fulfill the request of Preston and the South Carolina legislature. He read deeply in the history of Jeffersonian resistance to the Alien and Sedition Acts, congressional records, and treatises on the southern economy. After completing his research, Calhoun took two weeks to compose a thirty-five-thousand-word manuscript for two documents: an "Exposition" of the South's complaints and another document titled "Sundry Resolutions." The two documents together would become the *Exposition and Protest*, published anonymously in December 1828. In its defense of states' rights and in proposing a way to counteract federal power, Calhoun's primer on nullification "stretched normal states' rights constitutional ideology to an abnormal extreme."[35]

Calhoun wanted anonymity because of the nature of his arguments, but as one historian has remarked, "Calhoun's style, needless to say, was anything but anonymous."[36] The first part of the document denounced the tariff as unjust and arbitrary, in essence collecting and distilling the complaints that southern planters had voiced about the tariff policy during much of the 1820s. Calhoun buttressed his argument by adding that the tariff amounted to majority tyranny over a numerical minority. The southern states produced two-thirds of the nation's exports but constituted only a third of the national population. The statement marked the beginning of Calhoun's idiosyncratic theories of majority rule and tyranny against minorities, which he returned to later in his political career.

To this point, Calhoun could have safely proclaimed his thoughts under his name, but what followed represented a novel—and some argued seditious—interpretation of the Union itself. Taking cues from the Virginia and Kentucky Resolutions of 1798 and a host of more recent commentators and sources, Calhoun struck down the theory of divided sovereignty. The states and the national government exercised sovereignty, each in its own way, but they did not share sovereignty over the people. In other words, the states remained sovereign and the federal government exercised power under strict limits as articulated in the Constitution. Calhoun had become a strict constructionist. In sum, the sovereign states had entered into a compact in which they granted specific powers to the national government but retained all others as well as their original sovereignty as individual political communities. To Calhoun's mind, the federal government itself could not judge the constitutionality of its own legislation because it had a vested interest in preserving and expanding its own power. The states, then, acted as a check against the federal government's actions by reserving their collective rights and exercising their sovereignty through nullification. A convention of the states could then deliberate on the matter and either grant or deny the power in question.

Even in his articulation of a compact theory of government, Calhoun had not trodden too far from what any Old Republican might espouse as sound constitutional interpretation. He had hewed closely to Jefferson and Madison in the Virginia and Kentucky Resolutions of 1798. Here Calhoun departed from precedent by stating that any state could suspend the enforcement of, or nullify, a federal law it considered unconstitutional. At this point, the federal government had two options: it could suspend enforcement of the offending law, or it could call for amending the Constitution to grant the power in question. Nullification, Calhoun argued, provided the only means for a numerical minority to assert its rights against the majority. In practice, of course, nullification promised to reduce the nation to permanent political paralysis. More likely, it could lead to disunion. Calhoun's challenge to the nationalists transcended traditional states' rights political theory by advocating nullification. Surely a few nationalists must have read the *Exposition* and recalled the Hartford Convention and its fruitless effort to thwart the tyrannical minority of 1815, which they argued resided in the South and West.

The *Exposition and Protest* disclosed the fear that Calhoun and many of his contemporaries had over the changing American nation. The document portrays the South as a beleaguered section facing rapid and incomprehensible change. In its printed form, the *Exposition* weds the South to slave-based agriculture as an enduring economic system. Commerce and manufacturing might enter the South as ancillary economic pursuits, but Calhoun made clear that they would serve to aid in the expansion of the slave empire. An unpublished portion of the document, however, reveals Calhoun's fears for a South in which the future of slavery might face threat. In his disquisition against the tariff, Calhoun argued that protection—which would foster industrialization—would lead to the creation of a proletarian class that would remain subservient to the elites. Inequality would reign, as it did in Europe, where distinct classes had emerged within society. A "moneyed aristocracy" would control wealth, making "the poor poorer, and the rich richer." The rise of manufacturing and the use of protectionism to aid its growth would destroy the southern way of life. "After we are exhausted, the contest will be between the capitalists and operatives; for into these two classes it must, ultimately, divide society."[37] To combat the destruction of southern agriculture, and not incidentally, the system of slavery that made it possible, Calhoun proposed a variant of Martin Van Buren's alliance of planters and "plain Republicans." If northerners and southerners could unite, sectionalism would disappear, nationalism correctly construed would reign, and the nation would avoid the degradation of Europe, with its impoverished proletariat and wealthy capitalists. But the North had to sanction slavery and promise to leave it alone. The South, in turn, would provide the raw materials necessary for northern manufacturing. What Calhoun did not recognize, or refused to see, was that in the insidious bargain he proposed, he had merely substituted the millions of enslaved people in the American South for the working class.

Calhoun believed that his *Exposition* served as a moderating force against the hotspurs who threated disunion over the tariff. To his mind, nullification and interposition preserved the Union by providing a channel for the redress of minority grievances. It sought to protect the South against the demographic and economic disasters that threatened to reduce the section to subservience within the Union. The Northeast seemed ascendant in its transformation from a commercial society to a manufacturing powerhouse. The South needed an ally in its campaign to check northern supremacy. Perhaps the agricultural West, with the hundreds of thousands of settlers who had moved from the south Atlantic states, would join forces with their former neighbors. Certainly Andrew Jackson's rise to the presidency in 1828 boded well for the prospect. Moreover, the West had its own concerns with northeastern power, especially with respect to access to land on the frontier. The sectional balance of power within the nation by 1828—North, South, and West—seemed ripe for deal making. With whom would the westerners ally?

3

The West Asserts Its Power

ON DECEMBER 29, 1829, Connecticut senator Samuel A. Foot proposed that Congress should "inquire into the expediency of limiting for a certain period the sales of the public lands to such lands only as have heretofore been offered for sale, and are subject to entry at the minimum price."[1] Additionally, the senator proposed abolishing the surveyor general's office as an economizing measure. To Foot's mind, the supply of existing land for sale outstripped demand to the point that additional surveys would create an oversupply and drive down land prices. The next day, Missouri senator Thomas Hart Benton rose in opposition to the Foot resolution. Benton parsed no words as he accused his eastern colleague of seeking to "check emigration to the Western States." Foot shook his head no, but Benton continued. "The Senator from Connecticut shakes his head, but he cannot shake the conviction out of my head that a check to Western emigration will be the effect of this resolution." The idea had appeared before, Benton noted, most recently in the debate on the Tariff of 1828. During those deliberations, Richard Rush, the secretary of the treasury under the Adams administration, had "dwelt openly and largely upon the necessity of checking the absorbing force of this emigration, in order to keep people in the East to work in the manufactories."

No, Benton implied, Foot sought to do the work that Rush had proposed the previous year.[2]

Limiting sales to lands already surveyed would cause the collapse of the western land market, according to Benton, because only marginal lands remained. "What are the lands to which the gentleman would limit the sales?" Benton asked. "Scraps; mere refuse; the leavings of repeated sales and pickings!" No eastern family would move west to purchase these "miserable remnants" at the government's minimum price of $1.25 an acre. "The man that moves to a new country wants new land; he wants first choice; he does not move for refuse, for the crumbs that remain after others are served," Benton protested.[3] But this is what Foot desired, Benton implied again. Eastern congressmen had sought before to check westward expansion for their own selfish purposes. They had sought to reform land policy in a way that would slow the migration of Americans beyond the Mississippi. They had refused to survey millions of acres within the Louisiana Purchase while settlers waited for their chance at the national domain. Foot and his allies sought to stop migration so that the eastern manufacturing interests could keep people in the East to work in factories. Worried eastern politicians feared for their political clout in a nation under transformation by the forces of western settlement.

Benton spoke hyperbolically, but his remarks represented fairly the prevailing attitudes of the westerners he represented. The opening of the Twenty-First Congress brought the western land debate to the forefront of national politics, leading to a debate on policy that had been a decade in the making. Foot protested too much when he depicted his resolution as merely an inquiry into the wise administration of the public lands, for in fact the Connecticut senator had deeper political motives in seeking to retrench on western land policy. Foot and his northeastern colleagues scorned the newly elected president, Andrew Jackson, and the political coalition that elected him to office. They had watched aghast as Martin Van Buren's alliance of planters and "plain Republicans," including a significant number of westerners, secured victory for the general. To some observers, the election of Jackson foretold doom for proponents of John Quincy Adams, the American System, and nationalist politics. They feared that further westward expansion jeopardized their political and economic position. Moreover, easterners believed that the western states had benefited disproportionately from federal policy at the expense of the older members of the Union. Vermont representative

Jonathan Hunt exemplified their resentment when, two weeks before Foot proposed his resolution in the Senate, he introduced a measure in the House of Representatives to distribute public land revenue to the states according to population.[4]

The Webster-Hayne Debate began not over the tariff or internal improvements but over the seemingly innocuous issue of surplus government land in the West. Historians and contemporaries alike have depicted the Foot resolution as a "routine motion of inquiry," yet recent research reveals a more complex story that illustrates the significance of land policy to politics in the early republic. In actuality, the American System and land policy were intimately connected in the aftermath of the Panic of 1819. Foot's proposal gave voice to the deep misgivings among northeasterners that westward expansion would stultify the expansion of their own section, which had become increasingly wedded to industrialization and development. Likewise, westerners viewed the land issue against the backdrop of ten years of steady debate over the national domain and who would control its destiny—the hardy and headstrong emigrants who settled in the West or the politicos who controlled land policy from the nation's capital.[5]

For westerners like Missouri senator Thomas Hart Benton, the election of Andrew Jackson signaled victory for easy land in the West, a prospect that they had desired for over ten years. Benton rose to power as one of Missouri's first senators, a position he held for thirty years. His rise to influence took a curious and checkered trajectory. The young Benton first moved west after being expelled from the University of North Carolina for stealing money from fellow students. Disgraced, Benton moved to Tennessee, where he became an aide-de-camp to General Andrew Jackson of the Tennessee militia. Soon Benton would have to leave the Volunteer State after a barroom brawl with Jackson left the future president with a bullet in his body. Moving to St. Louis during Missouri's territorial days, Benton sought to establish himself in the new territory. Again, violence got the better of him when he killed a man in a duel. The prideful Benton always seemed to have too much to prove, too much honor to defend. Benton's pride cost him dearly. The lack of a formal education, lost as a consequence of his own indiscretions, haunted the man throughout his career. Nevertheless, in Missouri he stayed and became a successful lawyer, newspaper editor, and politician.[6]

Like many westerners, Benton faced financial ruin with the Panic of 1819.

Senator Thomas Hart Benton of Missouri. Benton portrayed himself as the champion of western interests, specifically the availability of cheap land for settlers. Benton played a crucial role in the debate because it started over a bill to limit the sale of western lands. Courtesy of the Library of Congress. Reproduction number LC-USZ62-71877

Speculation based on easy credit had ensnared many westerners who sought to make fortunes off of the land-buying bonanza. "The years of 1819 and '20 were a period of gloom and agony, spreading desolation over the land, and carrying ruin to debtors," Benton recalled in his memoirs.[7] When the boom went bust, men like Benton faced mountains of debt with little means to keep their good names. They blamed banking, specifically the Bank of the United States, for their woes. The collapse of easy credit led to hard times. The cry for relief thundered from western communities. Benton's instincts told him that a leader who could focus on the plight of the farmers could rise in politics. In the Senate, his agrarian proclivities drew Benton to the Old Republicans of Virginia, all of whom highlighted the competing sectional interests that they believed subjugated the tillers of the land to a second-class status.

Before Benton's entry into the Senate, Congress debated the Land Act of 1820, a reform bill designed to prevent speculation on western lands and reserve parcels for actual farmers. Congress lowered the maximum parcel to eighty acres and decreased the minimum price to $1.25 per acre. More important, Congress ended the practice of selling land on credit, which it believed had caused the land bubble that helped to create the panic. When President James Monroe signed the bill into law on April 24, 1820, many Americans believed that their representatives had upheld the Jeffersonian principles of agrarianism against rampant land speculation. Americans had a visceral connection to the farmer as a humble cultivator of the land. To the Jeffersonian-influenced mind, the Louisiana Purchase had promised future generations of Americans the ability to control their own destinies free from outside interference. The land speculator abused the system by hoarding parcels of land purchased on credit to make a windfall in the future. But the speculator produced nothing but paper wealth. And after the Panic of 1819, it seemed that his actions produced economic ruin.

Perception and reality diverged in the land issue and the causes of the real estate bubble that had popped in 1819. Western politicians like Thomas Hart Benton conveniently excised the details of how farmers speculated, too, as they purchased lands that they intended to sell in the future for a profit. They used credit, subsidized by the federal government prior to 1820, to secure title. Land speculation dominated the market economies of many western communities in a way that few Jeffersonians cared to admit. The speculator became a booster, a creator of frontier communities based on building demand for farms and the towns that would inevitably spring up in the western territories. More available land begat more speculation, which led to further expansion. Western prosperity, then, depended in no small part on speculation and the emigration that would boost prices in the long term. It also depended, especially after the land reforms of 1820, on the steady migration of middle-class Americans with sufficient means to purchase land with cash.[8]

By the early 1820s, the push for land reform by easterners led to a reaction among westerners who remained committed to liberal land policies. Many westerners resented the paternalistic land policies that placed the federal government in the role of an administrator of a West that required tutelage from Washington. Several different views developed over the course of the 1820s that transformed the debate over land policy and reveal sharp sectional differences between the North, West, and South. The debates also revealed an increasing class-consciousness among westerners, who realized that the government's cash-only land policy restricted sales to people of means. A more egalitarian approach, they argued, would open the availability of land to a wider segment of American society. Some westerners rejected the entire notion that the federal government should act as an agent for the sale of western lands. Others took a more moderate position, emphasizing that the government should sell the national domain at minimal cost in order to facilitate more rapid settlement and expansion.[9]

When he exclaimed in 1826 that "the public lands belong to the People," Senator Benton of Missouri spoke for a wide segment of the western population who sought to build a new vision for westward expansion that would decentralize power over land policy by deferring to the states.[10] Over the first half of the 1820s, Benton devised the components of a new land policy for the West that proposed to overhaul thoroughly the way in which the federal government administered public land sales. Spurred by concerns that westward expansion had halted amid the weak economic market, westerners like Benton proposed to reduce federal land prices. Western prosperity depended on the resumption of land sales and, indeed, speculation that spurred economic development on the frontier. The cries of westerners for relief, however, became entangled in simultaneous debates over internal improvements and tariffs.

That Americans would go to the polls in 1824 to elect a new president, amid a disintegration of political parties and a rise of factionalism that brought forth four candidates for the highest office, which complicated matters. So, too, did the significant differences over the course of westward expansion and the federal government's policy on western lands that emerged during the election season. Not only had the debates over the tariff and internal improvements become sectionalized, but the discussions over land policy also took on sectional overtones. The debate over the General Survey Bill of 1824 revealed how the American System could become entwined with western lands. The survey bill appropriated $30,000 to conduct surveys of roads and canals considered important for commercial and military purposes. Its author, a Pennsylvania representative, had written the legislation carefully to avoid constitutional objections, especially from the strict constructionist President Monroe. Fearing that the survey bill would usher in a new program of national internal improvements, the Old Republicans voiced their opposition. Sensing that public opinion was swaying toward internal improvements that would connect the West to the East, Virginia's agrarians marshaled a series of constitutional objections. A project's importance to national development did not make its execution constitutional, warned one Virginia congressman. Others argued that local governments, not the federal government, should pursue road projects. A new objection emerged alongside the older localist staples of the Old Republican guard: federal spending for internal improvements inevitably led to favoritism. Some states would receive more of the federal largesse than others, provoking jealousy among the states that gained less.[11]

When Henry Clay sought to blunt the criticism of his Old Republican colleagues by asking them to consider the plight of "the West, the poor West," John Randolph, the "dean of the Old Republicans," attempted to quell the rising western support for public works and cheap lands.[12] With palpable resentment, Randolph spoke on behalf of the Old Republicans, who feared not only the rise of federal power that would come with a general program of internal improvements but also the impact of westward expansion on the political and economic influence of the older states. "What have we done for the West? Sir, let *me* reverse the question. What have we *not* done for the West?" Randolph continued, asking Clay if he needed "monuments" to mark all the aid the East had sent west. Westerners could find them "in the Indian treaties for the extinguishment of title to lands—in grants of land, the effects of which begin now to be felt in Ohio, Kentucky, and Tennessee, as they have long been severely felt in Maryland, Carolina, and Virginia." Here Randolph sharply referred to the outflow of population from the south Atlantic states to the West that had alarmed him and many of his contemporaries. To them, westward expansion cost money, population, and influence. Moving on, the Old Republican urged Clay and the West to look to "laws granting every facility to the nominal payment and . . . for the spunging of, of the debts due the Government, by purchasers of the public lands." Once again, Randolph betrayed his resentment at western development by referring to the legislation passed since the Panic of 1819 that sought to foster western land development and provide debt suspension or forgiveness to straitened western farmers and speculators. Finally, Randolph noted that the federal government had offered generous land grants "which cannot be found in the older States" for public education.[13]

Clay gamely tried to rebut his Old Republican foe. "Sir, the Western States have never received any thing from this Government for which they have not given an equivalent. They have paid a *quid* for every *quo*." Clay need not have protested too much; the floor vote on the survey bill rebuked the Old Republican opposition. A coalition of the mid-Atlantic and western states banded together to secure the bill's passage in both houses of Congress. Virginia, the Carolinas, and Georgia joined New England in opposition.[14] More telling, however, and more troubling for the opponents of strict construction and consolidation was the fact that thirteen of the twenty-four state delegations to Congress supported the General Survey Bill, with its promise of federal aid to expansion and internal improvements. Along with the 1824 tariff, it seemed that the federal government had changed course toward a nationalist agenda designed to encompass the industrializing Northeast and the agrarian West. The remaining southern nationalists, including South Carolina's George McDuffie, joined in for the time being. Sectional differences and discord would soon change circumstances dramatically.[15]

Against the backdrop of the survey bill and tariff debates, in April 1824 Thomas Hart Benton introduced an early version of what become known as graduation, a policy that called for dynamic pricing of land based on the time a given parcel remained for sale. Good lands sold rapidly in the western markets, but less desirable tracts remained unsold. To alleviate the problem and to allow for a wider segment of the population to afford land, Benton called for a new minimum price of fifty cents an acre. An additional policy, clearly designed to favor squatters on the land, offered eighty acres of free land to any settler who lived on it for three years. Introduced late in the congressional session, Benton's plan had no chance of getting a floor vote, but he had planted the idea in Congress and staked his initial claim as the spokesman for cheap lands in the West.

The problem with graduation, as his fellow senator from Missouri and political enemy David Barton readily pointed out, lay in the fact that diminished land prices would strain the treasury. Undeterred, Benton worked hard to build support at home in Missouri and throughout the western states for graduation. Benton approached the task with zeal, for he had happened upon an issue that would win support in the western states. The legislature in Benton's home state of Missouri petitioned Congress to pass the graduation bill.

When the Nineteenth Congress convened in December 1825, Benton stood ready to fight for the yeomen of the West with a revised plan. In its second iteration, Benton's graduation policy reduced the price of parcels—at a rate of twenty-five cents per acre per year—based on the length of time they remained on the market. After five years, if the minimum price held at $1.25 per acre, the lands would become free to settlers who lived on the land for three years.

Just as Benton prepared to unveil his latest graduation plan, the Old Republican John Randolph offered, in a roundabout way befitting his idiosyncratic character, another option for the disposition of western lands. As Congress debated a bill on the Cumberland Road, to which Randolph vigorously objected as an unconstitutional reach by the federal government, he offered his "wish that every new State had all the lands within the State" so that they might not be "brought under the influence of this ten miles square," meaning Washington, D.C.[16] Had Randolph, the foe of westward expansion, really meant to suggest that the states should control the unsold lands within their boundaries instead of the federal government acting as the agent of the states? One might have dismissed the Virginian's remarks as yet another manifestation of his odd behavior except for the fact that the idea seemed to gain support from several senators. New York senator Martin Van Buren lamented that land policies had led the West to an "unwise and unprofitable dependence on the Federal Government." Better to "devise some plan by which the United States might be relieved from the ownership of this property, by some equitable mode."[17] Randolph's fellow Virginia senator Littleton Tazewell soon introduced a resolution on his absent colleague's behalf providing for just what Van Buren had suggested, the disposition of public lands to the states, but at his request the Senate took no action.[18]

Cession of federally controlled lands to the individual states gained little traction in the Nineteenth Congress, but it soon joined graduation as one of the two significant ideas for public land reform throughout the 1820s. The graduation plan, championed by Thomas Hart Benton of Missouri, would have boosted land sales by reducing the price of land parcels the longer they remained on the market. In the context of Old Republican ideology, Randolph's seemingly bizarre comment made sense. The Old Republicans may have opposed westward expansion, but they outright despised the nationalist policies that had emerged in recent years to spur economic development in the Northeast, via the tariff, and in the West, via internal improvements. By devolving control over public lands to the states, the Old Republicans could starve the beast; that is, they could perhaps cut incoming federal revenues to the point that the federal government, now under the control of the nationalist president John Quincy Adams, to the point that it could not support nationalist expenditures like road and canal projects that siphoned off eastern citizens and paved their path west. Westerners would soon take up the issue where Randolph had left off.

Benton took a different approach by pressing on with his graduation plan, surmising that it would have a better chance of gaining congressional support. For the Missouri senator, land reform lay at the heart of his Jeffersonian conception of political economy. Benton promoted what he believed would foster the growth of an agrarian republic of small freehold farmers, traders, and merchants unencumbered by concentrated wealth. The plan required an expansion of democracy and the availability of cheap land for the republic to reproduce itself across space. His was a vision straight out of the Jeffersonian mind. To that end, by 1826 Benton had adopted several political hobbyhorses: a constitutional amendment providing for the popular election of the president and vice president, opposition to national banking, and the graduation-donation plan. The constitutional amendment had no chance of advancing in a Congress with a majority of Adams supporters, but Benton's calls for land reform resonated with westerners desperate to reinvigorate their economy.[19]

Benton offered an impassioned statement in favor of graduation in the waning days of the Nineteenth Congress's first session. His speech in the Senate revealed just how much he had refined the plan over the previous two years. Perhaps most important, Benton had finally found his true audience, not in his Senate colleagues but in the thousands of westerners who saw the federal government as an overbearing landlord of the national domain. Yet Benton had to persuade his colleagues of the importance of land reform. Steeped in language sure to rally farmers but learned enough to impress solons, Benton defended his plan against those who believed that westward expansion had run amok. "I speak to statesmen and not to compting clerks; to Senators, and not to *Quaestors* of provinces; to an assembly of legislators and not to a keeper of the King's forests," Benton proclaimed. "I speak to Senators who know this to be a Republic, not a Monarchy; who know that the public lands belong to the People, and not to the Federal Government."[20]

Benton had seized upon the pent-up resentment of westerners who saw the East as a distant power that controlled the public domain in a quasi-colonial status. The president and Congress had adopted the notion that the lands served Washington as an inexhaustible cash generator rather than their true purpose: a generator of democracy on the frontier. Practical concerns, too, merited reform of the current land policy. Benton argued that the sale of public lands had not produced the desired effect of paying the national debt; indeed, revenue could not even meet the government's annual interest payments. Moreover, because the government set an arbitrarily high minimum price, regardless of the quality of the parcels, it had priced many people out of buying western lands. "No man will give one dollar twenty-five cents for a quarter section that has but one half, one quarter, or one tenth part of it fit for cultivation," he reasoned.[21] Without a steady stream of settlers moving west onto public lands, making improvements, and cultivating the soil, the government could never hope realistically for an increase in their value. The government then, by its own doing, had slowed the progress of western communities by adopting a policy out of touch with the realities of settling on the frontier.

Dynamic pricing of western lands would alleviate many of the problems inherent in the government's current policies by accounting for the quality of lands and allowing people to buy lands for different purposes. Benton used the example of a farmer who wanted to purchase a section adjoining his land because of its resources such as timber, stone, or water. Though the parcel was unsuitable for agriculture, the farmer would still have to petition the government to purchase the land at the exorbitant price of $1.25 an acre. Benton implied that the policy makers who devised the land policies in force had no idea of the real conditions on the ground in places like Missouri.

In sum, the federal government had proven itself unable to manage the western lands under current policy. That left Congress with two options. It could reform the policy or divest itself of the lands. Benton supported either arrangement but suspected that Congress would never support the latter option. Regardless, Benton believed that westerners should stand for states' rights and against current federal policy because the states themselves could better manage the public domain. Here Benton pivoted toward a bigger issue that loomed large in his mind. He had argued that current policy made poor economic sense because it cost westerners in terms of increasing land values and the federal government by stagnant revenue on sales. Population growth had slowed as well with the lack of credit and high minimum prices. "But it is not to wealth and population of the States alone, that the fatal effects of this

Federal dominion over their soil is extended," Benton argued. "It reaches and affects a still higher object—*the sovereign character of the States themselves.*"[22] The old states had possession of the lands within their boundaries, but the new states had an administrator—the federal government—that controlled a significant part of their lands and set rules sometimes at odds with state and local leaders. States' rights had crept into discussions of land policy.

Benton introduced his graduation bill too late in the session for Congress to take action, but he had achieved his goal of forcing the issue upon Washington and inflaming the spirit of the West in favor of real land reform. Moreover, he had laid the issue of land policy at the White House door. John Quincy Adams had won election in 1824 in no small part because a group of western congressmen had swung their votes in the House of Representatives to his column. Benton's arguments for reform, one observer noted, was "about as well calculated to prove that Jackson ought to have been elected president instead of Adams, as they are to show the utility of reducing the price of public lands."[23]

For his part, President Adams wanted to avoid the land issue at all costs. He realized that his election had hinged on key votes from the Northwest and that his reelection bid would require southern and western support. Yet he also realized that Benton had seized upon an important issue that would animate western voters and gain Benton power and influence. The president rationalized in his diary that "the best days of our land-sales are past" while predicting that "we shall have trouble from that quarter," meaning Benton and the West. Adams despised Benton as an opportunistic grasper who sought to inflame his constituents rather than serve them. The president believed that westward expansion would prove beneficial only if the federal government acted as an overseer, coordinating the sale of lands, the construction of internal improvements, and the coordination of the western farming economy with eastern commerce and manufacturing. In sum, he endorsed the American System and the patient, deliberate development of the federal domain over time. Yet politics made his position more difficult because Benton had indeed seized on an important issue that motivated westerners. John Scott, an Adams supporter and the chairman of the House Committee on Public Lands, recommended to Secretary of State Clay that the president adopt graduation as the administration's policy. Benton's plan "had stimulated all the people of the Western country to madness for the public lands" though he hastened to add that the Northwest had not adopted the radicalism of new states like

Missouri. Clay would have nothing of graduation or cession, seeing the senti-ments expressed in Senator Benton's speech as a resurrection of Aaron Burr's schemes to create a western confederacy—"treasonable in their character."[24]

Benton faced stiff competition for his campaign to become the spokesman of the West and its interests. Henry Clay had built his congressional career off of representing western interests, arguing that the creation of home markets would foster the growth of the agrarian West alongside the commercial East. To Clay, Benton's policies smacked of self-promotion and blatant sectional-ism. The West would prosper, the Kentuckian argued, as America prospered. "What is the best application of the aggregate industry of a nation, that can be made honestly to produce the largest sum of national wealth?" Clay asked in an 1824 speech on tariff legislation.[25] His answer was simple: Americans could celebrate their regional diversity, but for economic security they had to unite. Clay's American System provided the means to accomplish that end. Conversely, Benton's plan would squander the federal domain while creating a resource-poor population on the frontier that would take decades to climb out of poverty. The Panic of 1819 had proven that the West suffered from a dearth of capital for funding improvements. Without connections to eastern markets, western agrarians would languish in a regional economy that could not prosper. Clay's plan for national economic development, on the other hand, allocated resources in a way that created opportunity for the North, South, and West.

By the time Benton and Clay clashed over the future of the federal domain, four options had emerged for how to reform land policy. One option, which President Adams preferred and which fit with his vision for national eco-nomic development, called for the federal government to maintain its control of the public lands and use the revenue to fund internal improvements and education in the new states as well as the old. This option addressed a long-standing concern of easterners that land sales provided the new West states with funds for programs like education but did not afford the same benefits for the old states. Indeed, the plan to distribute revenue from land sales to the states that Vermont representative Jonathan Hunt proposed just prior to the introduction of the Foot resolution in December 1829 followed Ad-ams's preferences. A second option, similar in ends and slightly different in means, also addressed the concerns of the old states, especially with respect to education funding. During the economic depression of 1819, Virgil Maxcy, senator in the Maryland legislature, took issue with the educational grants on the Northwest Ordinance that provided funds for schools in the new states. Maxcy argued that the old states deserved a share of the profits from land sales. Instead, westward expansion had caused eastern land values to suffer as people migrated to the new lands. He proposed that Congress pass legislation to grant shares of the western lands to the new and old states so that all the Union could share equally in the federal domain. At the time, leaders in Maryland wished to create a common school fund with their share of the land profits. Their proposal, however, betrayed the intense sectionalism that land policy could provoke.

Some leaders, including Henry Clay, looked for other solutions that would quiet the bickering between the eastern and western states over land profits and quell the rising sentiment of sectionalism. Clay supported a third option whereby the federal government would distribute revenue from land sales to the states. Under this plan, the federal government would remain the agent for disposition of the public lands but would share the proceeds with all the states. The states, then, and not the federal government, could use the funds to suit their own purposes. Distribution gained support among more nationalist-minded Americans and seemed to offer a middle ground between strict and broad construction of the Constitution, but the Jacksonian Democrats later attacked the principle on the grounds that the federal treasury should not act as a funding source for the states. States' rights, after all, demanded that the states themselves care for their own concerns and not end up beholden to federal largesse.[26]

For states' rights advocates, especially those in the West and those who would come to form an important part of the Jacksonian coalition, a fourth option, cession of lands to the states themselves, provided the most attractive proposal. Cession was also the most radical option. Advocates of decentralization took several positions. Benton offered his graduation plan as a moderate approach to removing land policy from federal purview and empowering states and frontier communities to influence westward expansion. Graduation, however, did not suffice for some westerners. First as a US senator and later as governor, Illinois politician Ninian Edwards became the chief spokesman for cession during the 1820s. His attacks on the federal land system exhibited the growing populist uprising among westerners who saw their region as a haven for the poor and a place of ever-upward economic opportunity. The movement for cession also revealed the states' rights tendencies of westerners. Though westerners had benefited significantly from federal largesse, the

Panic of 1819 and the collapse of banking in the West had provoked strong feelings of resentment of centralized power. With Adams as president, states' rights westerners saw more threats to come as the agents of nationalism and consolidation sought to dictate policy from Washington. Men like Edwards intended to stop the Adams coalition and wrest control over the national domain from the nationalists themselves.

Cession gained traction beyond the mere mention it received in the Nineteenth Congress from Virginia's John Randolph. Westerners had become enthralled by the discussions over land policy and sought the means to assert their own sovereignty and authority. Thus matured the relationship between land policy and states' rights as westerners clamored against federal land policy, which they argued violated the principle of state sovereignty and equality. The cession idea itself matured, replete with constitutional theories that the federal government's ownership of the public domain violated the principles of states' rights and the Constitution itself. And the states' rights reaction against federal ownership of the public domain occurred at a time when the North was embracing and the South was distancing itself from nationalism.

The Adams administration hardly helped assuage western concerns about federal management of lands. Adams had tried to sidestep the public land issue only to face criticism when he defended current policy in his December 1827 annual message to Congress. Four days later, Secretary of the Treasury Richard Rush issued an economic report that included observations highly critical of land reform. Together the two messages further inflamed westerners who had embraced the calls for reform. "The system upon which this great national interest has been managed was the result of long, anxious, and persevering deliberation," Adams wrote to Congress. "Matured and modified by the progress of our population and the lessons of experience, it has been hitherto eminently successful."[27] Adams's remarks, however, ignored the situation on the ground in western states, where significant resentment toward land policy had blended with states' rights sentiment. An appeal to good government would not convince the supporters of Thomas Hart Benton or Ninian Edwards that the Adams administration had the welfare of westerners at heart. In private, the president held both men in contempt, but in his annual message Adams avoided outright condemnation of graduation or cession.

If the western radicals saw smoke in Adams's message, they saw fire in the Rush report. The treasury secretary might have sought to build bridges to the West by extolling the virtues of the American System to western farming interests, but Rush burned them when he implied that haphazard settlement in the West threatened the section's interests as well as eastern economic development. Regarding land policy, Rush noted, "The manner in which the remote lands of the United States are selling and settling, whilst it may possibly tend to increase more quickly the aggregate population of the country, and the mere means of subsistence, does not increase capital in the same proportion." He regarded the "diffusion of a thin population over a great surface of soil" as injurious to national development and encouraged any policy that "may serve to hold back this tendency to diffusion from running too far."[28]

In other words, Rush believed that the lands of the West offered a too-enticing prospect to easterners who sought to improve their lot in life. The East needed an enticement of its own to keep its population in place. For Rush, the tariff served those means because it assisted the expansion of industry and the expansion of employment for easterners. In one respect, Rush's logic made sense. Westerners had received federal aid through the national domain that propelled growth and development. Surely easterners deserved federal aid as well, in the form of protection for industry. Unfortunately for Rush and the Adams administration, the secretary's report seemed to suggest an either/or proposition rather than trying to balance the countervailing forces of agrarianism and industry, as Clay sought with his interpretation of the American System.

Before the rise of western radicalism on land policy, the comments of Adams and Rush would have elicited little significant criticism, but the proponents of graduation and cession had intensified the belligerent tone of western politics. They seized upon Rush's assertion that population diffusion wasted much-needed capital for eastern enterprise as evidence that the Adams administration opposed land reform, including especially the graduation and cession plans. Benton, however, had a grand strategy in mind as he denounced the Adams administration as an enemy of the West. The Missouri senator worked to forge an alliance between the states' rights, strict construction advocates of the South and West. Politically speaking, the alliance seemed at least plausible if not natural. By 1828, the South had largely united in opposition of protection because of how it drained southern capital. Moreover, they saw the tariff as part of a nationalist program that ceded far too much power to the federal government. Slavery, and its ultimate destiny, always loomed in the background. In the West, however, Benton found politics more complicated. The land reform radicals of Missouri, Indiana, and Illinois could unite behind calls for reform, but the American System complicated matters. By 1828, the maturing northwestern states had grown attached to protection of industry and federal aid for internal improvements in ways that the infant western states could not yet conceive or understand. The economy of the Northwest bore increasingly closer ties to the northeastern states, which made Benton's plan for an alliance between the South and West more difficult to achieve.[29]

Benton could, however, strengthen ties between southerners and western-ers by finding a common enemy in opposition to land reform and in support of protection. Forgoing cooperation from the northwestern states, Benton extended overtures to the South on the premise that the American System, as implemented by the Adams administration, posed a mutual threat to sec-tional interests in both the West and South. Cooperation had its issues, but Benton tried his best to curry southern favor by illustrating how land reform would provide much-needed revenue to pay the national debt and lower tar-iffs. In exchange, Benton called for southern support on graduation.

Westerners continued to move in the direction of radical land reform as the election year of 1828 dawned. The unpopular Adams faced a ground-swell of opposition from western states, fueled in part by antipathy toward nationalism. By 1828, leaders in six states and territories in the West had endorsed graduation. Leaders in Illinois and Indiana, however, pressed for the even more radical alternative of cession. In December 1827, Indiana sena-tor Thomas Hendricks introduced a resolution asking Congress to consider cession of the western lands. Hendricks recognized Benton's graduation plan and predicted that the Missourian would once again introduce legislation in the new session, but the Indiana senator believed that cession would better solve the economic issues of land policy by allowing the states themselves to adopt a policy of graduation. Moreover, cession would address the constitu-tional problems with the status quo, which had increasingly captivated states' rights proponents. Echoing the rhetoric of his fellow westerners, Hendricks argued that the current system had interfered with the "sovereignty, freedom, and independence of the new States" and that cession would address these issues better than Benton's version of graduation. "Surely," Hendricks argued, "the legislatures of the States are better qualified than the Congress of the United States, to dispose of the public lands, as the conditions of their respec-tive States require."[30] Not only could the states themselves better administer the disposition of lands, but they would also do better at graduating prices according to market realities.

True to form, Benton introduced graduation legislation four days after Hendricks offered his resolution in the Senate. But in the new context of western radicalism on land reform, graduation appeared far less radical than it had just a few years before. Benton's latest remarks on graduation suggested implicitly that cession could not garner support in the eastern states. Repeatedly, the Missouri senator stressed that graduation would benefit all the states, not just the new states of the West or the older states of the eastern seaboard. The political wrangling over cession versus graduation had commenced. Several weeks later, Hendricks offered a variant of his cession proposal as an amendment to Benton's graduation bill. He proposed that the federal government adopt Benton's policy for the territories, where the federal government had clear jurisdiction, and cede public lands in the states to the states themselves to alleviate the western states' "abject and humiliating dependence on the Federal Government."[31] Alabama senator John McKinley, who a decade later became an associate justice of the Supreme Court, joined in defense of the Hendricks amendment in an effort to bolster the states' rights argument against federal management of lands within the states. McKinley argued that the federal government had no right to own land in the states except as prescribed in the Constitution and that "whatever right they had to the soil while the country remained under territorial governments, passed to the States formed over the same territory on their admission into the Union, on an equal footing with the old States."[32]

The debate proceeded over graduation and the cession amendment, but it became clear that, true to Benton's sense of the situation, cession could not command sufficient support in the Senate. Many senators, especially from the Northeast, saw the proposal as too radical. On April 1, Hendricks withdrew his amendment and let graduation stand on its own for a vote in the Senate. Cession may have failed, but western sentiment remained strong in favor of land reform, which the senators could not help but recognize. Eight states and territories had sent memorials and petitions to Congress urging support for graduation. During the debate, however, the tariff issue surfaced as an additional issue when westerners addressed the Rush report and its remarks on protection. Benton's overtures for unity between the South and West were working.

When graduation finally came up for a roll-call vote, Benton's Missouri nemesis David Barton attempted to derail the plan by extending the period between land price reductions from one to five years. The amendment would have benefited land sales in the older western states while delaying price reductions in the newer states, a point that Benton recognized immediately. At this point, Benton made a brilliant political maneuver. Because the Barton amendment favored the older western states such as Ohio and Indiana over the new states in the Southwest, it would likely augment political power in the North and allow the creation of a free state long before a slave territory was ready for admission to the Union. Therefore, the amendment could throw off the delicate balance between free and slave states and shift political power. The mere mention of the slavery issue changed the character of the debate. When the Senate voted on the Barton amendment, the south Atlantic states and the West united in opposition, while the Northeast voted in favor. Of the twenty-five southern and western senators who voted, only David Barton himself voted for the amendment.[33]

After seven roll-call votes on various amendments, graduation failed in the Senate—twenty-one in favor and twenty-five against. Daniel Webster of Massachusetts expressed his support for some form of graduation, but not at the accelerated pace that Benton proposed. Webster, along with other New Englanders, feared that speculators would hoard the lands and that the plan would create an unwarranted land rush. Based on the previous votes on various amendments and his sense of the situation, Benton predicted that the New England and mid-Atlantic states would vote against graduation, which is why he needed the alliance between the South and the West. His alliance, however, failed in the final roll-call vote when John Tyler of Virginia, along with the four senators from the Carolinas, including Robert Y. Hayne, voted against the bill. Benton needed four of the five votes to carry the bill. In the end, the Missourian had come close to achieving his plans, but the southerners had failed to deliver on their end of the alliance. Then again, the ensuing vote on the Tariff of 1828—the so-called Tariff of Abominations—showed divisions in the West over protection. The southwestern state senators generally voted against protection, while the northwestern delegation supported the revised schedules.[34]

Westerners—radical or not—fumed at the outcome of the graduation vote, which had deprived them again of significant land reform. With near unanimity they blamed New England and the president who hailed from that section: John Quincy Adams. Election-year politics provided the backdrop for much of the anti-Adams agitation, with graduation as the westerners' preferred mode of attack. Whereas southerners launched their philippics against

Adams and the nationalists by denouncing the Tariff of Abominations, politicians from the West harnessed the farmers' discontent by keeping land policy in the newspapers. "Can there now be any doubt of the hostility of Messrs. Adams & Rush, *and their whole party in Congress*, to the adoption of any measure calculated to promote the prosperity or grandeur of the West?" a Missouri newspaper asked.[35]

On virtually every front, the Adams administration had floundered on domestic policy. Westerners excoriated the president on westward expansion, southerners seethed at the tariff, nationalists lamented that the American System had devolved into a political grab bag of favors to local communities and constituencies rather than a coherent plan for national development. Intersectional unity had eluded the politicians in Washington, a fact clearly illustrated by the mutual resentments aired by northern, southern, and western political and economic interests. A bitter campaign ensued between John Quincy Adams and Andrew Jackson, with each side leveling scurrilous accusations against the other. In many respects, the major issues that had coalesced in recent years gave way to a campaign of characters.

The Jackson campaign, under the adroit management of Martin Van Buren, worked hard to build the alliance of planters and "plain Republicans" that would dethrone Adams. The president himself hoped that the program of economic development and improvement that he supported would curry favor with voters beyond New England. True, the systematic nature of the American System had given way to petty regional competition, but the Adams administration had nonetheless overseen an impressive distribution of federal assistance to the different sections of the Union. In the end, Adams could not overcome the dissent that had beset his administration since its beginning. At the same time, Jackson's populist message resonated with voters. He carried the South and West as well as key votes in the mid-Atlantic states. Predictably, Adams won the New England states, but his success stopped there. The rise of popular politics and the spread of democracy had produced a backlash against Adams and his administration.[36]

In the western states, graduation had played a notable role in the outcome. Keen observers during the election season noted the significance of land policy to voters. Even Adams supporters in the western states had to avoid their candidate's opinions on land policy in order to garner votes in local and state elections. In July 1828, Daniel Webster offered a negative assessment of Adams's chances in Indiana, a hotbed of support for reform, where the people were "mightily taken with the project of graduating the price of the public lands."[37] Clearly the new states of the West saw the land issue as vital to their political interests and to the election itself. Adams offered nothing for them, and so, to a state, they turned to Andrew Jackson for a new direction.

The end of the election did not quite mark the crescendo of the radicals' charge for reform, as western governors maintained the pressure for reform even after Andrew Jackson's election to the presidency. In Louisiana, the push to transform the government's relationship to the national domain evolved quickly. The state legislature initially asked for the right of preemption and the reduction of prices for public lands, but after a sharp message from the governor in which he demanded graduation or cession, the legislature sent a second memorial demanding cession of public lands.[38] Mississippi echoed the complaints of its western neighbor. In January 1829, Missouri's General Assembly issued a statement calling for "a radical change in the system of disposing of the public lands," namely graduation and cession. In its memorial, the assembly argued that "hundreds" of the state's citizens had migrated to Texas. More ominously, the legislators argued that the slow pace of settlement had halted the progress of Indian removal within Missouri, leaving the state's frontier "exposed to the depredations of the restless hordes of predatory savages collected thereon."[39]

The governors of Illinois and Indiana remained fervent in their calls for land reform, but some observers questioned their motives. Illinois governor Ninian Edwards became the most outspoken and most controversial supporter of cession. A veteran politician in his adopted home state, Edwards had served as territorial governor for nine years. After a stint in the US Senate, Edwards returned home in 1826 to serve as governor. Like Benton, Governor Edwards seized on the land issue as key to maintaining power within the state by criticizing the arbitrarily high minimum price that the government levied on all lands regardless of quality. The Rush report galvanized his opinion against the Adams administration and its land policy. The governor's demands culminated in a blustery speech to the Illinois legislature in December 1828. Adopting the language of the Old Republicans who attacked centralized authority, Edwards called for the cession of public lands to the states on the grounds that the states could better administer the lands within their sovereign boundaries than could the federal government. Edwards went far beyond his fellow western radicals, however, when he declared the federal land system null and void within the state of Illinois. To this point, westerners had merely argued for congressional reform, but Edwards made the assertion that absent action from Washington the western states could and should take matters into their own hands by nullifying federal land policy and seizing control of the public domain.

Edwards laid out an argument that bore more than a faint resemblance to the words of John C. Calhoun, who at that very moment labored in his home on the South Carolina *Exposition and Protest*, which became known as a seminal defense of the doctrine of nullification. The document, which made the legal and constitutional case for the nullifiers' opposition to the Tariff of Abominations and defended the right of nullification, appeared in print anonymously just a few weeks later. Edwards's own speech to the Illinois legislature outlined a case for the protection of minority rights. If the federal government would not exercise its duty to administer the public lands as delineated in the original acts of cession by the states, then the states themselves had the right to take charge. After all, Edwards implied, the Tenth Amendment guaranteed sovereignty to the states within their own limits on powers not expressly granted to the federal government. Any federal exercise of authority, or the lack thereof, that restricted the power of the states was "not only voidable like civil contracts made during infancy, but absolutely null and void as being incompatible with, and repugnant to the fundamental law." Finally, Edwards threatened to sue in federal court in an effort to void federal title to the lands if Congress would not agree to cession.[40]

With good reason, some observers questioned Edwards's motives in pushing so hard on the land reform issue. The Illinois governor had his eyes set on returning to the US Senate and saw land reform as the means to achieve his goal. Veteran political operative and newspaper editor Duff Green agreed with Edwards's argument for cession, stating that the western states should have the "right of soil" if they had equality with the old states. But Green also recognized that the land issue resonated with westerners, and for that reason the newspaper editor encouraged Edwards to press forward, though he predicted that any appeal to the Supreme Court, then under the leadership of the venerable Federalist John Marshall, would end in failure. "My own advice is to press your land question, get up and continue the discussion in the newspapers of your own and the other Western states," Green advised. "Make yourself the head of that measure, and you will be forced into the Senate."[41]

Regardless of Edwards's true motives, his strategy of building support for a radical vision of cession worked in the near term. Indiana's state legislature soon followed with its own call for cession and an effort to ally with six other western states to adopt resolutions in favor of the Edwards proposal.[42] In the coming five years, three states followed the lead of Illinois and Indiana by calling for cession. Yet something rang hollow in the complaints of the western states. At the very moment that state legislatures called for radical land reform, they asked Congress time and again for land grants, reduction of land prices, and the right of preemption on public lands. In sum, the record suggests that even the more radical western politicians saw cession as a far-fetched scheme for reform.[43]

Whether they actually believed in cession or used it as a way to bargain for more moderate reforms, it soon became clear that the radicals had overplayed their hand. Congress showed little interest in the proposals for cession or for the grasping politicians who supported the idea. The issue simply could not gain a broad coalition of support when far more moderate measures appeared feasible. More to the point, plenty of congressmen, even some from western states, stood ready to illustrate the hypocrisy of the extreme states' rights position on the western lands issue when so many new western states relied on federal munificence for land grants and relief legislation. During the debate on Thomas Hendricks's amendment to Benton's graduation bill, Indiana senator James Noble rebuked his fellow Hoosier senator by asking why he—and the Indiana radicals—called for cession while asking for graduation and preemption. Alabama senator John McKinley offered thanks for a congressional land grant for river improvements while arguing for the state's right to claim all public lands within its boundaries. Congress moved to shut down the cession debate promptly, even refusing initially to print the Indiana state legislature's memorial demanding cession. Easterners, in particular, had grown weary of western radicalism and sought to quiet the discord that in many ways mirrored the emerging crisis over the tariff.[44]

Eastern congressmen believed that distribution, whereby the federal government would distribute revenues from land sales to the states based on population, would quiet the debate over graduation and cession. When it was first introduced in the mid-1820s, westerners had seemed at least open to the idea because it promised to mitigate high land prices by returning a portion to the states, which they could use for internal improvements. In the new political atmosphere, in which westerners had called for more radical solutions to their issues, distribution offered far too little relief. Easterners would continue to benefit from land sales at a disproportionate rate to the newer states because the eastern states still had larger populations. Of course, the eastern proponents of distribution recognized this fact.

Pennsylvania representative James Stevenson, chairman of a select committee called to investigate distribution, made clear his goal of ending the interminable debate over radical western policies in his report to Congress on the distribution plan. Whereas Duff Green spoke to Ninian Edwards of the "right of soil" belonging to the states themselves, Stevenson countered in his report that "the indisputable *right of soil* yet remains in the United States."[45] If left to western designs, Stevenson argued, the states would sell the vast national domain at a fraction of its worth and in an unorganized manner that would inhibit the orderly growth and development of the frontier. Devolving control of land sales to the states would create multiple systems that might often be at odds with one another. More important, Stevenson, an ally of the Jackson administration, argued that graduation or cession would end the progress made on eliminating the national debt. The public lands served as a fund for repaying the nation's debt; thereafter, they could provide a bounty for the states to conduct improvements as they saw fit.

The Stevenson report betrayed the exasperation of easterners with the radical, states' rights vision of the western governors who called for cession, but it also revealed the problems with a nation continually beset by sectional jealousies and differences. In his report, Stevenson made a crucial distinction between local interests and national unity that would gain greater meaning in the following year when Webster and Hayne began their debate in the Senate. "The patriotism of the citizens of the old States," Stevenson wrote, "who voluntarily conceded these lands to the *Union*, might here be placed by the committee in strong contrast with the want of that feeling in the citizens of the new States who could seriously demand from the Union the surrender of all this valuable property *to them alone*."[46] His remarks implied that a national union did exist for the benefit of the people of all the states and that the federal government should have authority over some matters that impacted all American citizens. The states could not administer the public domain in a way that would benefit the nation. The founders had recognized this fact and had promoted the cession of state lands to the federal government for that very reason. Now, almost fifty years later, western radicals sought to undo a system that had served the people well. States' rights, Stevenson implied, had their limits.

Though Congress failed to act on Stevenson's proposal, the message against western radicalism did not lay on the table. By the end of 1829, it became clear that the citizens of the old states had no stomach for the wild propositions of men like Ninian Edwards or even Thomas Hart Benton. Cession and graduation, the former permanently and the latter for a time, had died. Land reform had drawn support from the new states of the Northwest and Southwest, but now as the tariff issue became increasingly important, western politics changed subtly. The southwestern states like Louisiana and Mississippi saw a twin threat in federal land policy and the Tariff of Abominations. Both revealed a strong national government dictating to the states. The Southeast, however, became uneasy as it appeared that northwestern states like Ohio generally supported protection. The southern-western alliance that Benton had sought to build for his graduation proposal showed its weaknesses on the eve of Andrew Jackson's inauguration as president.

In his first annual message to Congress, John Quincy Adams encouraged Congress to embrace public improvement as a program of nation building. "Let us not be unmindful that liberty is power; that the nation blessed with the largest portion of liberty must in proportion to its numbers be the most powerful nation upon earth, and that the tenure of power by man . . . shall be exercised to ends of beneficence, to improve the condition of himself and his fellow-men."[47] Whereas Adams saw the national government as the agent of change that would use its power to achieve greater liberty, Jackson and his followers saw liberty and power as antithetical. Centralized power, they believed, would restrain, if not trample, liberty. To a New England manufacturer, the federal government's power to offer protection to industry produced greater liberty. To the southern planter, however, that same power diminished liberty. Likewise, residents of the old states looked at federal land policy as a means of directing westward expansion toward greater ends, toward a coordinated effort to expand across space and over time. Westerners, however, saw the power to control land policy as a check on their freedom and liberty to expand as they saw fit. In these terms, liberty and power themselves had become sectionalized. The power to improve the lot of people in one part of the Union cost the residents of other regions liberty. Adams's belief that "liberty is power" rested on a broader vision of national unity than most Americans shared in the late 1820s. The continuing debate over land policy, which in 1829 morphed into a discussion on the nature of the Union, proved the elusive nature of national unity.

4

The Great Debate

On January 26, 1830, Massachusetts senator Daniel Webster took the rostrum in the US Senate to deliver the speech that defined him as a defender of the Union. The forty-eight-year-old senator, impeccably dressed in his oratorical costume, spoke for three hours on that day and almost as long the next, delivering a volley of rhetorical blows against those who had calculated the value of the Union and threatened nullification and disunion. He artfully led his debating opponent—South Carolina senator and pro-nullification leader Robert Y. Hayne—into delivering a discourse on union and disunion that in some ways strayed from the issues at hand in the initial deliberation. The maneuver gave Webster the opportunity to define his nationalist conception of the Union. The people, not the states, had breathed life into the Union. This interpretation, which he so dazzlingly characterized in the speech, culminated with a phrase that school children memorized for generations thereafter, "Liberty *and* Union, now and forever, one and inseparable!"[1]

The "Godlike Daniel," an appellation bestowed on the senator by fans of his speechmaking, choreographed his oratory carefully. Webster, like many early American politicians and leaders, honed his craft on audiences in an era when constituents expected long (if sometimes long-winded) declamations on the issues of the day. To practice politics well meant to connect with

G. P. A. Healy, *Webster Replying to Hayne* (1851). Healy's work, which captures Daniel Webster delivering his second reply to Robert Hayne, hangs above the rostrum in the Great Hall of Faneuil Hall in Boston. Courtesy Boston Art Commission 2017

audiences on the speaking circuit. For Webster, who had left audiences spellbound before, his greatest moment of oratorical fame up to this point in his life came with the death of John Adams in 1826. The Boston city council called upon Webster to deliver a public eulogy in historic Faneuil Hall just two months after the second president's death. Such a public oration called for careful preparation, and Webster did not disappoint. He spent days poring over the archives of the Massachusetts Historical Society; after all, his audience would expect a thorough and well-researched account of the elder Adams's life and work. The kind of eulogy Webster planned to deliver, one that was not uncommon at the time, demanded exhaustive research on the subject's life and his significance to American life. That two of America's founding fathers had died the same day, John Adams and Thomas Jefferson on Independence Day 1826, lent greater gravity to the occasion. After the preparation and research came the composition of the address, which seemed almost anticlimactic after the intense research. Years later, Webster recalled that he "wrote that speech one morning before breakfast, in my library, and when it was finished my paper was wet with my tears."[2]

The Adams eulogy reveals many of the rhetorical devices that Webster would use with mastery in his debate with Robert Y. Hayne. At Faneuil Hall, Webster had the tear-stained manuscript at his side, but not once did he refer to the sheaf of paper. He intoned the words "Let those doors be opened," and the funeral procession advanced into the venerable old hall where so many of Massachusetts's leaders had addressed the people of Boston. Dressed in the brass-buttoned blue coat that became his "orator's gown," as he called it, Webster recalled the events of Adams's life. He spoke, briefly, of Jefferson, who had died within hours of Adams's own demise. But a mere account of a life would not suffice; orators in the early American republic often resorted to detailed history lessons to give meaning to a topic, or in this case, a life. As a Founding Father, Adams merited a eulogy that taught the audience about his contribution to American ideals and American republicanism. Though Jefferson had authored the Declaration of Independence, giving voice to the ideals of the Revolutionary generation, Adams had provided a quiet, forceful eloquence that strengthened the document and its author. Here Webster worked to a soaring conclusion—another characteristic of his oratory—that encapsulated the qualities of Adams's eloquence and patriotism: "The clear conception, outrunning the deductions of logic, the high purpose, the firm resolve, the dauntless spirit, speaking on the tongue, beaming from the eye, informing every feature, and urging the whole man onward, right onward to his object—this, this is eloquence; or rather it is something greater and higher than all eloquence, it is action, noble, sublime, godlike action."[3] The words must be spoken to achieve the address's full effect on Webster's audience, but by now the "Godlike Daniel" had the audience in his hand. And here Webster pulled one of the greatest sleights of hand in early American oratory: he invented a conversation between John Adams and an opponent of the Declaration of Independence during the summer of 1776. The audience, rapt with attention just as the eulogist had intended, felt the dead man personified in Daniel Webster. At the speech's end, two and a half hours after it had commenced, a hushed audience filed from the hall. And then the letters of congratulations came pouring in for Webster. He had ascended to the peak of American oratory.

Webster possessed the power to transform a eulogy into a declamation on American patriotism, and four years later in the Webster-Hayne Debate, he would use those powers to transform a debate that began over western land policy into a meditation on the meaning of the Union. Webster seized the moment not to debate the finer points of land distribution, as Samuel Foot and Thomas Hart Benton had, but to address what he saw as the underlying conflict behind all the contested policies of his day: whether the Founders had created a confederation of sovereign states or a nation of people united behind a common government. Webster advanced a nationalist interpretation of the Union against Hayne's extreme states' rights doctrine. Indeed, the major difference between Webster's famous second reply to Hayne and his eulogy of John Adams stems from how the audience received the material. Addressing the throng of mourners in Boston, Webster sought to reinforce the belief in American patriotism that he knew his audience shared. In his second reply to Hayne, Webster pushed the boundaries of the people's ties to their nation, just as Hayne had pushed the idea of nullification beyond its limits. Understanding Webster's and Hayne's divergent ideas of union brings greater clarity to the issues that Americans faced in 1830 and restores a sense of how they interpreted those issues through the lens of constitutional theory.

In the aftermath of his debate with Robert Hayne, Webster remarked to a friend that the "whole matter was quite unexpected."[4] Webster told only half the truth; though he may have come upon Hayne's speech by happenstance, the senator had looked for over a year for an opportunity to address the incendiary doctrines of nullification coming from the Palmetto State. Since the publication of Calhoun's *Exposition and Protest*, Webster had feared that the explosive rhetoric could threaten the harmony of the Union. Moreover, Webster deplored the definition of union coming from the Carolina hotspurs because he had a very different conception of what kind of nation the founders had created. Now Webster saw an opportunity to solve an age-old debate in the United States. Early nineteenth-century Americans did not agree on the nature of the Union: was it a confederation of sovereign states or a federal union made up of smaller political entities governed by a strong national government? Calhoun, Hayne, and the nullifiers subscribed to the former; Webster adhered to the latter.

Nationalists and states' rights advocates may not have agreed on the nature of the Union, but politicians across the spectrum recognized that the growing West had a role to play in the debate. Northerners and southerners alike agreed that the rapidly growing West and its population likely held the balance of power in determining the direction of the nation's politics. Indeed, Webster and Hayne—and their followers—saw the West as the fulcrum of their political programs. Northerners and southerners believed that their political destiny hinged on how westerners sided on the three interwoven issues of economics, public lands, and states' rights versus nationalism that emerged during the debate. The deliberations over Samuel Foot's resolution on the public lands had revealed western hostility toward the commerce-oriented Northeast and its leaders who sought to put the brakes on rampant westward expansion. That said, the recent debates over internal improvements and credit had also shown that westerners and southerners did not always share common interests; westerners needed dollars for improvement and credit to expand their fledgling economy. Discerning where westerners would side led both Webster and Hayne to speak to the section and its leaders during the Webster-Hayne Debate.

Thomas Hart Benton positioned himself as the spokesman of an aggrieved West in the debate over the Foot resolution, which had indeed offended many westerners who sensed a northeastern plot to halt the growth and development of the frontier. As shown by the intemperate remarks of western politicians like Illinois's Ninian Edwards, various forms of nullification were in the air not only in the South but in certain western quarters as well. The rhetoric continued beyond the end of the presidential election, with the advocates of cession even resorting to veiled threats against the Union to secure an acceptable change in policy. The 1829 message of the Illinois Assembly to Congress attacked the "present oppressive system," arguing that Congress had jeopardized "the control of the internal concerns and police" of a sovereign state. The assembly offered the veiled threat of seizure if Congress did not take steps to ensure Illinois the "essential attributes of its sovereignty"—namely, cession of federal land within the state.[5]

Benton opposed Edwards and his threats to nullify federal authority over the public lands in the West, but the Missourian did not hesitate to ensure that Andrew Jackson's election in 1828 would result in easier terms for western land policy. Far from resting on the laurels of victory, Benton had "stoked the fires of sectional animosity" throughout the first year of Jackson's administration in a bid to forge an alliance of southern and western states that would lend his section the crucial support it needed to promote a liberal land policy.[6] The Missouri senator's initial remarks on the Foot resolution, delivered the day after the Connecticut senator offered his proposals, reiterated claims he had made before. Arguing that Foot had taken up an "old and favorite" policy of northeastern politicians to stem the growth of the western states and territories, a clear effort "to check emigration to the Western states," Benton again chastised easterners for threatening westward expansion and continuing the antiexpansionist politics of the Adams administration. Reaching the height of hyperbole, the senator argued that the "young West had been saved from an attempt to strangle it in the cradle" by southern allies who would once again partner with the West to check the Northeast's agenda.[7]

Three weeks later, on January 18, Benton delivered what historians consider the first entry in the Webster-Hayne Debate. In this second caustic rebuke of Foot's resolution, Benton reiterated his accusation that northeasterners threatened western development for their own purposes. "The proposed inquiry is to do wrong; to inflict unmixed, unmitigated evil upon the new States and Territories," Benton thundered on the Senate floor. Foot's resolution proposed to limit land sales to those parcels already surveyed by the government. Benton scoffed at the policy, especially because it was antithetical to his favored policy of graduation, where the government would gradually lower the prices of unsold lands relative to their time on the market. Suspending land sales in the West to unsold lands that he called "the refuse of forty years picking under the Spanish government and twenty more under the Government of the United States," would prove "eminently injurious to the rights and interests of the new States and Territories" and, Benton predicted, would lead to "the greatest dissatisfaction of the new States in the West and South."[8] Moreover, the federal government had already obtained legal title to the lands from Native American nations and had provided for their removal. Halting sales, then, would lead squatters to settle illegally on the lands while the federal government suspended the survey. This problem, plus the impracticality of abolishing the surveyor general's office itself, would lead to confusion and anarchy on the frontier—and all for no good purpose.

Throughout the speech, Benton portrayed Foot as the spokesman of the northeastern manufacturing interests and an ardent opponent of western interests. Such labels, however, did more to obscure the varied interests of northeasterners and westerners. Branding New England with the stigma of antiexpansionist sentiment made sense if the Missouri senator wanted to achieve his goal of a southern-western alliance. So too did portraying the West as an agricultural region with few connections to eastern industry. In actuality, both statements generalized too neatly. Few observers disputed that Samuel Foot opposed westward expansion, but the notion that the Connecticut senator represented the mind-set of his section gave an inaccurate impression of the Northeast's attitude toward the West. Much had changed during the 1820s, and by decade's end many New England manufacturers and merchants realized that the West provided crucial home markets for the goods they produced and sold. Likewise, westerners in older states like Ohio had developed close connections with eastern manufacturing and industry that complicated politics.[9]

No matter to Benton, however, who seized upon the moment to build bridges to the South's leaders. At first glance, forging ties between the two sections made perfect sense because both southerners and westerners spurned the manufacturing Northeast—not only on the issue of public lands but also on the tariff. The relationship, however, was not without its complications. First, Benton had actually voted in favor of the Tariff of 1828—or as southerners called it, the Tariff of Abominations—in part because the exhaustive schedules created through the debate promised protection for the Missouri lead-mining industry. Benton maintained that he opposed a protection system that favored the Northeast, but like many politicians he consistently voted for measures that benefited his constituency. Those yea votes, however, could have proven problematic at the moment that Benton attempted to forge ties with the South. But Benton skillfully linked the tariff and land policy as evidence of a northeastern plot to subject the West and South to manufacturing interests. Both, according to Benton, would prevent westward migration.

Other political issues also threatened the alliance. Westerners had traditionally supported internal improvements because they desperately needed transportation development yet lacked the necessary capital. Benton himself had endorsed public financing for roads and canals in an effort to stimulate western development. Because many southerners had jettisoned their nationalist tendencies over the course of the 1820s in favor of the Old Republican creed of strict construction and states' rights, they argued that the American System inequitably and unconstitutionally drained southern economic resources. Tariffs paid by the South, they argued, paid for the roads and canals connecting the East with the West. Southerners footed the bill for the enterprise with little to show for their investment, as few projects made their way into the southern states.[10]

Some New Englanders mused that westerners would reap greater economic benefit from supporting Foot's resolution than by endorsing Benton and his policies of cheap and abundant land. Supply far outstripped demand, which depressed prices but had also led to the seemingly counterintuitive consequence of slowing westward migration. With land prices so depressed,

eastern citizens saw little value in purchasing lands and making improvements that would not yield a return on their investment through resale. Fur-
thermore, surveying and selling additional public lands would result in more
haphazard and diffuse settlement on the frontier, a problem that Benton
acknowledged and claimed that his graduation plan would mitigate. How,
though, asked northeastern observers, would the availability of even more
land achieve the goal of more compact and orderly settlement?[11]

Economic complexities aside, Benton's diatribe against the Northeast drew
the interest of southerners, who sought to claim advantage for their section
in the battles over land policy, the tariff, and internal improvements. Northeastern support for restrictive land policy and crippling tariffs revealed the
section's true colors, they argued. Quoting Thomas Roderick Dew's "Lectures
on the Restrictive System," Benton argued that "these tariff measures injure
the South and West by preventing that emigration which would otherwise
take place." Foot's resolution to halt land sales in the West only exacerbated
the problems caused by the tariff, which ultimately would reduce the poor
population of the East to wage slavery. So when Benton called for assistance
from "the ancient defender and savior of the West," his cries did not go unanswered.[12]

On the day following Benton's speech, South Carolina senator Robert Y.
Hayne responded to Benton's overtures and offered his section's support for
the beleaguered West. Hayne, thirty-nine years old, smart, articulate, and
eager to rise even further politically, had become an able spokesman for
the Palmetto State hotspurs. First elected to the Senate in 1822, Hayne had
emerged even before then as an able politician with sterling connections.
Hayne had allied himself with key Palmetto State leaders through business
associations and marriage into two of South Carolina's first families. Hayne
had first entered the political world as a protégé of Langdon Cheves, a wealthy
Charleston lawyer and former director of the Bank of the United States. He
assumed control of his mentor's law firm when Cheves won election to Congress in 1812. One year later, he married the daughter of Charles Pinckney,
former governor of South Carolina, member of the Continental Congress,
and a wealthy low-country rice planter. When she died in 1819, Hayne remar-
ried—this time to another woman from an influential and wealthy family.
Small wonder, then, that Hayne entered politics himself by 1814.

Hayne's star rose further when, in 1822, South Carolina sent him to the

South Carolina senator Robert Young Hayne in the early 1830s. Hayne championed the South Carolina nullifiers' vision of states' rights in the Senate. By the end of 1832, he resigned to become governor of South Carolina and stand against the threats of Andrew Jackson to crush the nullifiers. Courtesy of Wikimedia Commons

nation's capital as one of its two senators. He became a vocal opponent of the tariff and a defender of the South's peculiar institution against outside interference. Like Calhoun, he had once endorsed nationalism only to become disillusioned with national development in the ruinous years of the 1820s. Calhoun replaced Cheves as the young senator's mentor, and Hayne became increasingly allied with the vice president and his ideas. But where Calhoun possessed a brilliant theoretical mind in terms of political philosophy, Hayne saw politics as more of an applied science. The difference became apparent when Hayne spoke in the Senate and would continue to appear during the Webster-Hayne Debate.[13]

In speeches after his reelection to the Senate in 1828, Hayne expressed palpable resentment toward the North and its economic and political pre-eminence. "Viewing the United States as one country, the people of the South might be considered as strangers in the land of their fathers," Hayne charged in a speech against the tariff. He charged that the "fruits of [southern] indus-try" had flowed north while the benefits of union had "in a great measure ceased."[14] Clearly influenced by the ideas of men like Thomas Cooper, who had encouraged southerners to calculate the value of the Union to their inter-ests, Hayne and his Senate colleague William Smith gave voice to the anger of the nullifiers. Like Calhoun, Hayne and the nullifiers believed that the South had become an oppressed minority in a nation rushing headlong into indus-trialization. Slave-based agriculture had become the defining characteristic of the southern economy—and to a significant extent its social and cultural life—which increasingly alienated it from dominant northern interests.

The Van Buren alliance of planters and "plain Republicans" seemed to promise safety for southern interests, but the northern wing of the emerging party dashed the nullifiers' hopes when they supported the tariff schedules of 1828. And when Andrew Jackson indicated a lack of interest in renegotiat-ing the Tariff of Abominations, southerners like Hayne lost hope that their friends to the north would come to their assistance. The alliance survived in the long term, but in the immediate situation southern antitariff advocates had to turn elsewhere for assistance—to the West. Westerners wanted cheap land, and southerners wanted a tariff that would only produce the revenue sufficient to maintain the federal government's operations. The arrangement seems self-evident, but politics complicated matters.

Hayne linked the plight of the South with the West by delivering a speech that connected the western lands issue with southern antipathy toward the tariff. Both sections, he argued, suffered at the hands of a meddling national government beholden to northeastern interests. As the spokesman for the low-country South Carolina aristocracy who detested the tariff as a manifes-tation of overweening federal power, Hayne transmitted to the Senate a mes-sage of resistance to federal power. Some observers sensed more than a hint of influence from Vice President John C. Calhoun, who had just recently writ-ten the *Exposition and Protest* anonymously for the South Carolina legislature.

Though Calhoun's authorship remained a secret for the moment, all knew of his opposition to the tariff. Perhaps Hayne spoke for the vice president, who had recently abandoned his nationalist principles in favor of a states' rights outlook designed to protect the South against the growing northern influence. In terms of the speechmaking, Hayne seemed to fall in line with Calhoun's ideology. Hayne had likewise taken up a unique—and extreme— version of states' rights ideology ascribed to the South Carolina nullifiers. Traditional Jeffersonian states' rights advocates called for the clear division of sovereignty between the federal government and the states that preserved the doctrine of localism but would never brook the extreme measures that Calhoun and his followers advocated. The nullifiers, most of whom were na- tionalists during the post–War of 1812 era, violently reacted against their erstwhile principles in favor of states' rights. By utilizing an obstructionist form of politics, they mirrored the Jeffersonian-era Federalists who had tried to block the Louisiana Purchase and the embargo against France and Great Britain prior to the War of 1812 by using a narrow interpretation of the Con- stitution against the will of the majority. They had also asserted the right of states to review the constitutionality of federal law. Such logic came easily to Calhoun, who had maintained close ties to the Federalists before his political conversion. The Palmetto State's junior senator followed suit.[15]

South Carolina served as an example of how nationalism gave way to local- ism during the 1820s. In the years following the War of 1812, the state had embraced nationalism, with Calhoun as one of the leading spokesmen for national development. By the mid-1820s, however, South Carolinians aban- doned their nationalist credentials amid a severe economic crisis within the cotton economy. While the rest of the nation emerged from the Panic of 1819, the South—and especially South Carolina—languished amid depressed com- modity prices. Growing fearful for their economic security and their place of prominence within the Union, an internal struggle emerged within the state's body politic. Internal improvements, one of the main components of the American System, served the manufacturing interests at the cost of the agri- culturalists. Palmetto State politicians responded by withdrawing support for national public works projects, which they soon deemed unconstitutional on several grounds. Following the strict construction interpretation of the Old Republicans, southerners noted that the Constitution gave no express power to the government for internal improvements. Moreover, federal support for internal improvements meant that some people paid for projects that benefited others. Ever skeptical of the commercializing Northeast, southerners opposed to the American system claimed that the federal government favored industry over agriculture by funding internal improvements. Behind all the rhetoric against national economic development, however, lay a more serious concern. South Carolina's powerful slaveholders had begun to fear federal interference with their peculiar institution based on a series of developments in the early 1820s. A series of nationalist Supreme Court decisions that favored business interests plus the lingering anger over the Missouri controversy led many southerners to view federal power as a threat to the peculiar institution. Strict construction of the Constitution and limited federal power, they argued, was the only way to prevent interference with slavery.[16]

Increasingly, southerners viewed themselves as an embattled minority in a nation that had strayed from the tenets of Jeffersonian agrarianism. South Carolina, with its aristocratic politics and its planter oligarchy, harbored these feelings with the greatest intensity. Amid the turbulence in his home state, Calhoun, who had staked his political future on the buoyant postwar nationalism, gamely adhered to his principles until he could no longer ignore the direction of his constituency. In 1828, the South Carolina legislature asked Calhoun to draft a statement explaining the rationale and process by which a state could nullify federal law. In response, Calhoun anonymously wrote the *Exposition and Protest*, which argued that the South had become a political minority within the Union and that the northern majority sought to control the federal government. Like traditional states' rights proponents, Calhoun argued that the Union was a compact among sovereign states that had ceded only specific powers to the national government. But Calhoun diverged from them on the solution. Traditional states' rights proponents believed secession the ultimate remedy in only the most extreme cases when the federal government had exceeded its constitutional authority, usurped the rights of the people, and threatened the citizens' liberty. Calhoun, however, argued that a state could avoid secession by negating the offending law itself. The federal government, then, could either refrain from enforcing the law or initiating the process of constitutional amendment to secure the powers in question. Calhoun's concurrent majority counteracted numerical majorities by empowering the states as constitutional arbiters. In doing so, and in spite of his own protests to the contrary, Calhoun had created a new strain of states' rights that exceeded the Kentucky and Virginia Resolutions of 1798, the classic statements on states' rights ideology in which Thomas Jefferson and James Madison urged the states to resist the Alien and Sedition Acts.[17]

When Hayne approached the rostrum on January 19, then, he came not only with a strong opposition to the tariff, internal improvements, and federal interference with slavery but also with a broader ideological argument that sought to insulate his section from the nation's political majority.[18] Hayne began by making an overture to Benton: federal land policy had indeed injured the interests of the West. The West, according to Hayne, "had some cause for complaint" over the stifling regulations of that "hard taskmaster," the Northeast congressional delegation. Hayne led the Senate in a brief history lesson on land policy. Since the colonial era, he argued, settlers had obtained land for "a penny or a pepper corn," which had allowed for the rapid settlement of the frontier.[19] With settlement came independence and prosperity for those who moved west. Cheap land had provided the basis for the expansion of America in space as well as in affluence. Now, Hayne argued, northeasterners like Foot sought to curtail westward expansion for their own purposes.

Though Hayne agreed with Benton's depiction of the Northeast as an impediment to western growth, the South Carolinian did not agree with his Missouri colleague's proposed solution. Hayne offered measured support for a modified version of Illinois governor Ninian Edwards's radical plan to cede federal lands to the states. The senator, however, stated his preference that cession wait until the treasury retired the national debt. Apparently states' rights had its limits when it came to the disposition of public lands. Hayne had ulterior motives for delaying the cession. The loss of western land revenues would leave the federal government in need of revenue to pay down the national debt, which would likely come from higher tariffs.

Hayne saw the specter of corruption looming over the debate on Foot's resolution. The federal government, working at the behest of northeastern business interests, had become greedy in wringing every dollar it could from the frontier. At one time, Hayne argued, the government had administered a land policy that served the people. Now its policy had strayed from its original purposes by making "the cardinal point of our policy, not to settle the country, and facilitate the formation of new States, but to fill our coffers by coining our lands into gold."[20]

Now Hayne linked the plight of the West to the circumstances his own section faced. The South and West, Hayne argued, suffered "parallel oppressions" from a common foe: the American System, which subjugated agricultural interests to the northeastern manufacturing oligarchy. Grasping for full effect, Hayne likened the plight of his section to the Irish struggle against an overbearing Great Britain. The American System, he cautioned, relied on "a low and degraded population" to serve as the laborers for industry.[21] No wonder, then, that the Northeast sought to drain wealth from the South to feed its own interests and likewise aimed to prevent the flow of laborers to the fertile lands of the West. The South Carolinian forthwith launched into an attack on the tariff and on the northeastern manufacturing interests who demanded protection at the expense of southern planters. Greed for revenue had likewise led the federal government to plunder the South via oppressive policies. Hayne remarked that "the present condition of the Southern States has served to impress more deeply on my own mind, the grievous oppression of a system by which the wealth of a country is drained off to be expended elsewhere."[22]

With the case made against the industrializing Northeast, Hayne had only to define its purposes. Excoriating those who sought "consolidation" at the expense of the "independence of the States," Hayne laid bare the fears of southerners, especially his South Carolina brethren. The National Republicans—those Federalists under a new name—intended to subordinate the West and South to their ow purposes. Nationalism portended not a nation of sovereign states but a nation of dependencies held in control by a central government. Now infused with the nullifiers' own version of states' rights, Hayne's address led to a conclusion implicit in its text and unmistakable in the minds of his southern allies. If the federal government could impose a restrictive land policy, if it could impose high tariffs that enriched one section at the expense of another, it could impose its will on slaveholders and their human property.[23]

Hayne himself, however, pointed to the limits of an alliance between the South and West, one that had much to do with the unique interests of both sections and with the nullifiers' own emerging theories on state sovereignty. Hayne may have responded favorably to Benton's overtures for an alliance, but the South Carolinian also delineated its limits. Western politicians had floated many ideas for providing cheap land for settlers, including Benton's own policy of preemption and graduation. Preemption guaranteed a first settler the right to purchase a particular parcel of land at the government's minimum price. Graduation discounted the price on land parcels based on the time they sat unsold on the market until they reached a minimum price of fifty cents an acre. Southerners, including Hayne, believed that preemption and graduation favored settlement of yeoman farmers who inclined toward antislavery sentiments. The South, it becomes clear, had its own concerns with westward expansion. With preemption and graduation unsatisfactory and cession "untenable," according to Hayne, few options remained. What, then, did Hayne propose to satisfy the westerners? "I do not profess to have formed any fixed or settled opinions in relation to it," Hayne admitted.[24]

Other practical considerations beyond land policy further complicated a proposed political alliance between the South and West. Hayne may have lacked an opinion on the land issue, but he had strongly unfavorable sentiments on western calls for federal aid to internal improvements. Hayne chastised westerners for their unceasing calls on the federal government for "petty and partial appropriations" for internal improvements. "I am astonished," Hayne observed, "that gentlemen from the Western country have not perceived the tendency of such a course to rivet upon them for ever the system which they consider so fatal to their interests."[25] By the speech's end, Hayne seemed less interested in concrete solutions for western grievances and more interested in promoting the crusade of his own state and section against the tariff—and the American System as whole.

Hayne's prevarication on questions crucial to westerners illustrated the limits of an alliance between West and South. In theory, the alliance could have worked on the simple fact that the former wanted tariff relief and the latter wanted liberal land policies. Together they could accomplish both goals. The realities of sectional politics and local interests, however, complicated matters to the point that any alliance would be short lived. In spite of Benton's and Hayne's best efforts to ignore the matter, the interests of many westerners, especially farmers in the Northwest, meshed with those of the mid-Atlantic states. Internal improvements in transportation between the regions and tariffs that protected emerging home markets served western interests better than could any alliance with the southern states. Tariff policy had become a bewildering mess of local and regional compromises designed to placate political and business interests. Benton proved susceptible time and again to demands for protection, in spite of his insistence that he opposed protection. The latest example came in 1828 when Missouri lead miners and trappers insisted on duties that would protect their industries.[26]

Differences between the old and new Wests further complicated the prospects of a political alliance with the South. At one time, the older states stood in lockstep with the frontier states for land reform, but by the late 1820s differing interests reflected in the regional economies of the old and new West provoked telling divisions. In Ohio, for example, advanced development and strong connections to commercial interests in the Northeast changed economic priorities. Foot's resolution to suspend the western survey would have helped Ohio by closing frontier lands to development and slowing migration from the Old Northwest. The budding manufacturing interests of Ohio, like the commercial interests of New England, had no interest in losing population to the western frontier. By decade's end, Ohio stood for the American System and against easy migration to the far West.

South Carolinians shared more in common with the prevailing attitudes in Ohio than might seem apparent. Though politicians like Hayne may have been loath to admit it, the south Atlantic states such as South Carolina shared a common fear with the northeastern merchants they despised: the drain of population to the West threatened the economic vitality of both regions. A liberal land policy injured not only New England manufacturers but also southern economic interests. Moreover, the drain of population from the south Atlantic states to the Southwest had helped to create the atmosphere of fear in which South Carolina politicians lamented the decreasing influence that their state—and indeed their region—held in the halls of power. Exhausted soils on the Atlantic seaboard had pushed agriculturalists to the western frontier, where the promise of fertile lands at affordable prices proved too enticing. Opportunity for settlers came at a cost to the political establishment in the older states. Hayne's own failure to offer solutions for the land question betrayed the fact that southerners did not necessarily share the western zeal for cheap public lands.[27] In the short term, though, both Benton and Hayne recognized that an alliance served their immediate interests of blaming the manufacturing Northeast for the twin evils of an oppressive tariff and the restrictive land policy.

While Hayne began his diatribe against the tariff and stumbled toward building alliances with western politicians, Daniel Webster sat one floor below in the Supreme Court's chambers conducting business on behalf of a wealthy client. The high court prepared to hear the case of *Carver v. Jackson*, and Webster represented the millionaire New Yorker John Jacob Astor in the case. Finally, he gathered his papers under his arm and walked upstairs to the Senate chamber "just to see what was passing."[28] As he entered the room,

The west front of the US capitol in 1831. The old Senate chamber where Hayne and Webster sparred is located in the north wing of the building. Courtesy of the Library of Congress. Reproduction number LC-USZ62-113224.

Robert Hayne launched into his philippic against the Northeast. At the conclusion of Hayne's speech, a trio of Webster's colleagues, two from the New England states, approached him, stating that the South Carolinian's charges could not go unanswered. Webster agreed and resolved to write a rebuttal that he planned to deliver the following day.

In Webster's account, his involvement in the debate seems like happenstance. In actuality, he had taken keen notice of Benton's and Hayne's speechmaking. Though historians have often portrayed Webster as disinterested in the public lands debate, he had heard and addressed Benton's complaints before. Like many New Englanders, Webster believed that the western states and territories suffered from too-rapid development and a lack of social order. Better to slow the opening of lands in order to foster manageable growth than to allow opportunistic elements to control the destiny of the frontier. As Webster would define the issue fifteen years later during the debate over Texas annexation, "You have a Sparta; embellish it!"[29] In terms of policy, then, the senator opposed Benton's graduation plan and supported the principles behind Foot's resolution, in keeping with his calls for more orderly development.[30]

On this day, however, Webster cared little about engaging in a debate on public lands with Benton. He sought bigger quarry. Hayne's remarks on the bane of internal improvements, his cries against consolidation, and his impassioned call for states' rights, however, particularly captured Webster's interest. Just the previous day, Webster had endorsed—at Hayne's request—a bill for federal aid to the South Carolina Canal and Railroad Company, a short line designed to connect Charleston with the Savannah River. Webster must have instantly sensed the hypocrisy of a man who had just decried internal improvements and New England consolidation after asking a Massachusetts senator for assistance in securing federal dollars for a local project. Moreover, Webster surmised that Hayne also spoke for the vice president, John C. Calhoun, whose *Exposition and Protest* had alarmed the Massachusetts senator. The states' rights philosophy emanating from the Palmetto State ran counter to Webster's own evolving views on the nature of the Union, which emphasized economic and political nationalism. Hayne opened the door to a discussion of states' rights and nationalism, and now Webster intended to close the door on nullification.[31]

By responding to Hayne's intemperate—and to his mind, duplicitous—speech, Webster detected an opportunity to vindicate New England as an exemplar of the Union and a better friend of the West than the South had ever been or could ever be. To achieve this goal, however, Webster needed to address two issues. First, he had to cast off the pall that had hung over New England politicians since the abortive Hartford Convention of 1815 and the largely inaccurate accusations of southerners and westerners that the Northeast had considered disunion. New Englanders continued to chafe under the looming memory of the Hartford Convention and the alleged disloyalty of the Federalists during the War of 1812. The party had disintegrated after the war, largely because of the rumors of what happened at Hartford in 1815. Second, Webster had to prove that the greatest threat to westward expansion and American economic prosperity stemmed from southern opposition to the American System and the nullifiers' peculiar interpretation of states' rights. Webster had to illustrate the folly of a West-South alliance and show why the West's interests meshed with those of the Northeast.

Defending New England against the charges of disloyalty and self-interest, however, would not suffice to achieve Webster's ultimate goal, because the Massachusetts senator sought nothing less than to articulate an ideal of nationalism that he believed his section exemplified. Indeed, in both of his replies to Hayne, Webster portrayed nationalism as a "beleaguered national tradition" imperiled by the proponents of states' rights. To accomplish his goal, Webster would have to rewrite the history that Hayne had outlined in his initial speech and create a new narrative that emphasized the bonds between Americans and the states in which they lived. Since 1815, New Englanders had defended themselves against the charges of disloyalty and disunion. Now, with the South Carolinians raging against the federal government, threatening nullification, and perhaps implicating worse consequences, Webster could shift the blame away from his section and toward a legitimate threat to union.[32]

Accordingly, Webster ignored Thomas Hart Benton and his harangue on the Northeast, instead focusing his efforts on a counterattack against Hayne and the nullifiers. Most historians have argued that the Massachusetts senator wished to dispatch the issues of public lands as soon as possible in order to focus on the danger of Calhoun and Hayne's extreme version of states' rights and the promise of nationalism as envisioned by New England. In fact, Webster addressed the issue of western land policy so he could simultaneously attack the nullifiers as well as the western land cession contingent, whose pronouncements pointed toward a similarly harsh states' rights constitutional interpretation. An alliance between South and West could only embolden state sovereignty advocates in both sections and further imperil Webster's vision of national union.[33] Webster bristled at Hayne's impassioned defense of the South and its past and resolved to present his own version of American history, one in which New England played a pivotal role in the formation of nationalism and national character. The Massachusetts senator began with a measured endorsement of the Foot resolution largely on the grounds that the surplus of public lands for sale had created an environment for speculation, an argument that surely reminded observers of the painful effects of the Panic of 1819.

After addressing the resolution directly, Webster moved on to Robert Hayne. The South Carolina senator had argued that the Northeast had conspired to stem westward expansion for its own sectional interests. Webster flatly denied the charge, calling the government's land policies "a liberal and enlightened system."[34] Webster did not simply refute Hayne's charges; he argued that New England had actually authored and supported judicious land policies often against the wishes of the South! Webster cited the Northwest Ordinance as the greatest example of northeastern interest in westward expansion and praised one of Massachusetts's own sons—Nathan Dane—as its author, a claim that provoked controversy. During the 1820s and 1830s, as settler communities north of the Ohio River matured, citizens of the Old Northwest came to celebrate Dane as the author of the text, while southerners argued that their own Thomas Jefferson had crafted the legislation.[35]

Northerners and southerners sought to reorient history to portray their respective sections as exemplars of the American spirit, and Hayne would pounce on Webster's version in his reply to the Massachusetts senator. Webster pressed on, eager to defend New England against the charges that it had sought to stifle westward expansion. Just as Webster crafted his own narrative of westward expansion, he also offered a revised history of the tariff in an effort to weaken any potential alliance between the southern and western states. Webster reproached his colleague for blaming the protective tariff on the manufacturing Northeast when in actuality the South had pushed for duties in the aftermath of the War of 1812. To Webster's mind, Hayne had crafted a disingenuous argument to cement ties between southern and western interests. He used Ohio as his example of how the federal government's western land policies had fostered progress on the frontier, an especially apt selection since by the late 1820s, the Buckeye State had become an ardent supporter of the American System and a skeptic about Benton's graduation plan. Then he compared Ohio's success to Kentucky's rough beginnings and argued that the presence of slavery had weakened emigration south of the Ohio River.[36]

Webster's words on the slavery issue surely irritated Hayne and his southern colleagues. His history of the Northwest Ordinance led to a brief but forceful defense of antislavery sentiments in the states of the former territory. New England's wisdom, Webster argued, freed the Old Northwest from slavery "in original compact, not only deeper than all local law, but deeper also, than all local constitutions," and opened settlement for a vast emigration of freemen from the East.[37] The implication that the ordinance of 1787 transcended local law and state constitutions offended southerners, who feared any semblance of federal authority over the peculiar institution. Yet Webster moderated his comments by making clear that he believed the federal government could not touch slavery in the states. Webster's point served his purpose to weaken further the ties between the South and West by identifying the interests of the East, including antislavery, with the West.

In terms of the overall debate, the second part of Webster's speech, in which he outlined his conception of nationalism and union, became the most important part. During his discussion of land policy and the tariff, Webster lamented that South Carolinians like Hayne and Calhoun had abandoned nationalism in favor of states' rights. Illustrating that economic nationalism had once prevailed in the Palmetto State served his goal of identifying nationalism as the true American tradition. Webster returned to the point, reserving much of his thunder for Hayne's attack on consolidation. "Consolidation!—that perpetual cry, both of terror and delusion—consolidation!" cried Webster. While some southerners endorsed Thomas Cooper's famous declaration that, in Webster's words, it was "time to calculate the value of the Union" because of the "evils, real and imaginary, which the Government under the Union produces," northeasterners had stood at the vanguard of a government that had provided innumerable benefits to the nation and its development.[38] The American System had fostered western development in ways that Webster promptly enumerated. The federal government had provided for the orderly settlement of western lands in parcels that even Americans of limited means could afford, it had provided for educational opportunities through land sales, and it had built roads and canals that connected farmers on the frontier to eastern markets. An incredulous Webster pounced on Hayne's supposition that consolidation weakened the Union. "Can there be nothing pure in government, except the exercise of mere control?" Webster asked. Through his impassioned defense of federal action, Webster reminded the West that federal munificence had helped Americans settle the West. "Whatever is positively beneficent, whatever is actively good, whatever spreads abroad benefits and blessings which all can see, and all can feel, whatever opens intercourse, augments population, enhances the value of property, and diffuses knowledge—must all this be rejected and reprobated as a dangerous and obnoxious policy, hurrying us to the double ruin of a Government, turned into despotism by the mere exercise of acts of beneficence, and of a people, corrupted, beyond hope of rescue, by the improvement of their condition?"[39] Webster's consolidation, a vision that he linked to the nationalist vision of George Washington, had built a stronger nation. The Massachusetts senator had skillfully deflected criticism of the East while taking issue with the South—not the West. The West needed New England's vision of national union, he implied, because the South would not provide the assistance necessary for development and expansion. Here Webster elucidated a theme that he expanded on in his second reply to Hayne: the federal government was an agent of positive power that could secure the blessings of liberty and general welfare for future generations, not the agent of consolidation and oppression that Hayne and his colleagues deprecated.

Historians have recognized that Webster's first reply to Hayne cleverly steered the South Carolinian into a debate on the nature of the Union—and in particular, nullification. The entire chamber knew that the honor-bound Hayne would respond to Webster's comments against the nullifiers. So, too, did the public, which thronged the Senate chamber to hear the spirited forensics. Spectators packed the modest galleries of the Senate chamber; still others joined the senators on the floor. One observer claimed that three hundred women filled the aisles and spaces around the senators' desks. Some senators found themselves without a chair.[40]

Thomas Hart Benton, incredulous that Webster had ignored him throughout the speech, demanded the floor to offer a rebuttal himself. While Benton railed against Webster, the Massachusetts senator rushed to the Supreme Court chambers to secure a postponement of his pending case. Hayne waited patiently for his chance, which came after about an hour of posturing by the bombastic Missourian, who countered that Thomas Jefferson, and not Nathan Dane, had authored the antislavery provision of the Northwest Ordinance. Few cared, however, because the audience of solons and spectators recognized that Webster had accomplished his goal; by marginalizing Benton and engaging Hayne, he had shifted the debate toward a deliberation on the meaning of the Union itself.

Hayne did not disappoint once he began his address; over two days on the Senate floor, he railed against Webster's version of history and offered his own remarks on New England's past.[41] Hayne had three objectives for himself. First, Hayne sought to discredit Webster and his characterization of New England by portraying his Massachusetts colleague as a committed Federalist and a poor historian. Second, he had to defend nullification against the charges Webster had leveled against the theory. Calhoun shared Hayne's objectives, for the vice president had a stake in Hayne's success as well. He presided over the debate from a chair above the rostrum and may have even passed notes to Hayne encouraging him to make particular points during his speeches.[42]

Hayne made note of Webster's sleight of hand in which he avoided replying to Benton and instead charged against the South. The "Honorable Gentleman from Massachusetts . . . comes into this chamber to vindicate New England" by impugning the honor of the South, Hayne alleged, and "pours out all the vials of his mighty wrath upon my devoted head."[43] Webster's comments about slavery and the South provoked a stern response from the honor-bound Hayne, who sensed that the Massachusetts senator had ulterior motives. Comparing the settlement of Ohio to that of Kentucky rankled Hayne, who believed that Webster might have broached the topic to justify federal intervention with slavery as a positive benefit to westward expansion. Hayne remarked that he "could discern the very spirit of the Missouri question" into the debate, a reference that would have alerted any nullifier or Old Republican to the threat of federal intervention with slavery in the territories. Any "gentleman of mature age and experience" who made such incendiary comments "making war upon the unoffending South" must have "some object in view that he has not ventured to disclose," Hayne stated to the Senate.

Inveighing against Webster's section, Hayne reintroduced the oft-repeated cry of "Hartford Convention!" to his audience in his own clever way. Webster had lauded Nathan Dane as the purported author of the Northwest Ordinance, but Hayne retorted that the South knew Dane as a participant in the 1814 convention that had called for radical changes to the American compact. "So much for Nathan Dane of Beverly, Massachusetts," Hayne scoffed. Hayne would return to the Federalists of New England after he had attempted to dismantle Webster's statement about slavery and its effect on the South.

Hayne's rejoinder began well but trailed off as he continued. The South Carolinian showed that he had surmised Webster's game. But when Hayne transitioned to a discourse on the benefits of slavery, he lost sight of the importance of the debate as transformed by Webster's reply. He took offense at Webster's comments on the South's peculiar institution and defended chattel bondage against the nascent abolitionists of the North. No one could doubt, Hayne argued, that slavery "has never yet produced any injurious effects on individual or national character." The abolitionists of the North, however, intended to cause great harm to the Union and the southerners whose society rested in large part on the presence of African slavery. Webster's attacks on the South betrayed his true attitude toward southerners. Likewise, Webster's attacks on slavery proved that the Northeast held the South in contempt. Of course, to Hayne's mind attacking slavery crossed a line that no northerner had the right to cross.

The "meddling statesmen" of the North, according to Hayne, had long attacked the South. The oppressive tariff of 1828, which Webster supported, was the culmination of a trade policy that favored the northern states at the expense of the South. Hayne especially relished attacking Webster's changing position on protection, indicting him for endorsing free trade during much of the 1820s, only to support the Tariff of Abominations in 1828. "By that act," Hayne charged, Webster had "destroyed the labors of his whole life, and given a wound to the cause of free trade, never to be healed." He railed against the American System as a conglomeration of "wild and visionary projects, which can have no effect but to waste the energies and dissipate the resources of the country."

Finally, Hayne concluded with a ringing defense of the Carolina doctrine—as Webster had called it—but only after he assailed Webster and the Federalists for their disloyalty at Hartford. Hayne repeated the oft-leveled charges against New England that its people had abetted the enemy in a time of war. "At this dark period of our national affairs, where was the senator from Massachusetts?" Hayne asked. "How were his political associates employed? 'Calculating the value of the Union?'" Hayne reveled in throwing Thomas Cooper's words at the New England Federalists, whom he portrayed as the actual apostles of disunion—not for the righteous purposes of upholding the Constitution but for mere economic benefit. His silence was implicit recognition that Webster himself followed the tenets of New England Federalism—Hartford Convention and all.

Now Hayne made a tactical error that undermined the entire speech: he sought to defend nullification against the Webster assault. The South Carolinians offered nullification as a means of preventing disunion while upholding states' rights, he argued, a principle in complete continuity with the Virginia and Kentucky Resolutions of 1798.[44] "The history of disunion," Hayne said, "has been written by one, whose authority stands too high with the American people to be questioned—I mean Thomas Jefferson." After discrediting the Federalists for considering disunion, Hayne now presented nullification as the means to seek redress against grievances without sundering the Union. Yet many contemporaries believed nullification could and would indeed lead to disunion.

Hayne's greatest mistake, however, came in his description of the Constitution's genesis. The senator claimed that the states as well as a central government had together created the nation's charter. Any states' rights advocate would have noted the error immediately: adherents to the doctrine believed that the states alone had consented to the creation of a national government. Webster, who took careful notes during Hayne's entire presentation, noticed the error. So, too, did Vice President Calhoun, who would be forced to repudiate Hayne's comments in the so-called Fort Hill address of July 1831, in which he defended the doctrine of nullification and state sovereignty. Calhoun's statement, actually an essay published in a South Carolina newspaper rather than a public address, officially revealed the open secret that Calhoun had articulated the doctrine of nullification in the *Exposition and Protest* almost three years earlier.

Webster intended to reply instantaneously, but fortunately for him, the late hour of the day provoked a motion to adjourn. The senators had received Hayne's effort well, though they may have disagreed with its message. Thomas Hart Benton heaped praise on his southern ally. Edward Everett, a congressman from Massachusetts and a Webster associate, praised Hayne's address as "a very masterly effort, and delivered with a great deal of power and with an air of triumph."[45] The triumph would be fleeting, however, for Webster wasted no time in preparing his final reply to Robert Hayne. "I will grind him as fine as a pinch of snuff," Webster told Supreme Court Justice Joseph Story.[46]

If John C. Calhoun had heard Webster utter those words to Justice Story, he would have been inclined to agree. Calhoun rued the error that Hayne had made regarding the creation of the Constitution. The vice president and another southern senator, James Iredell of North Carolina, recognized too that Webster possessed rare talents that he would bring to bear in his reply. The South Carolina senator may have given a forceful address, but as Iredell remarked to a friend who praised Hayne's effort, "He has started the lion—but wait until we hear his roar, or feel his claws."[47]

Webster had succeeded in forcing Hayne to make nullification—rather than western lands or tariffs—the centerpiece of his speech. Now Webster had to respond with as much force and fervor as the South Carolinian had offered in his two-day speech. "I do not propose to let the case go by default, and without saying a word," Webster told his friend Everett at the senator's home that night.[48] Justice Story joined Webster for an evening of research to refute Hayne's claims. Meanwhile, Webster prepared for what would become the most celebrated speech of his career by arranging for Joseph Gales, the nation's premier stenographer, to transcribe the speech for publication. Gales, the editor of the *National Intelligencer*, had largely retired from stenography to focus on his newspaper but agreed to take up pen and pad for Webster's speech.

By now, the Senate debate became high political theater in an age when people prized oratory as good politics and better entertainment. The morning would find the Senate chamber filled with spectators waiting to see the "moral gladiatorship," as one senator's wife described the event, between Hayne and Webster.[49] The scene, splendidly recorded in G. P. A. Healy's 1851 painting that hangs in Boston's Faneuil Hall, reflects the interest that Washington observers had in Webster's coming speech. Dressed in his oratorical costume, brass-buttoned blue coat, buff-colored vest, and white cravat, Webster stood in the well of the chamber to deliver his second reply to Robert Y. Hayne. The dark, piercing eyes that so many people found enchanting canvassed the room of observers. The black hair, receding from his forehead and combed neatly to the side, would soon stand in a shock as Webster repeatedly ran his hand across the top of his head. Vice President Calhoun gazed down from the presider's chair, awaiting the lion's roar. The drama of the scene might have disappointed had Webster not prepared his words so carefully. And then, he quietly uttered the first words of the speech that immortalized him as the greatest American orator.[50]

For two days, Webster snared his quarry in the clever trap he had set by appealing not to Hayne, not to the Senate, but to the American people. Webster could not help tweaking his colleague for mistakenly alluding to William Shakespeare's *Macbeth*, which he turned into an opportunity to jest Hayne and Calhoun. Hayne had tried to connect Webster with the corrupt bargain of the Adams-Clay "Coalition" that had brought Adams to the presidency and made Clay the secretary of state. Webster dismissed the suggestion that the memory of any corrupt coalition had kept him awake; he had slept well the night before. But Hayne had erred, as it was the enemies at which Banquo's ghost would not down. The honest Banquo would not disturb an innocent man. And the ghost of the alleged Adams-Clay coalition did not disturb Webster. A specter would disturb Hayne and his mentor Calhoun, though, because they had strayed from the truth with their fanciful dreams of nullification. Webster stared at Calhoun as he finished revising the allusion, revealing that he surmised the true identity of the mind behind nullification.[51]

The beginning of his speech tread familiar ground, as Webster refuted many of Hayne's arguments point by point. Webster denied that his comments on slavery implied anything more than admiration for the Northwest Ordinance and his support for its stricture against slavery in that territory. Webster meant no threat to slavery, and yet Hayne "represents me as making an onset on the whole South, and manifesting a spirit which would interfere with, and disturb, their domestic condition!" Hayne's imagination had run wild, Webster implied. Next, Webster briefly turned once again to the West, denying that New England had ever sought to prevent expansion. He also defended internal improvements, using them as an example of how a nation could become stronger when united behind common interests and goals. "We look upon the States, not as separated, but as united," Webster stated on behalf of New England. "We love to dwell on that union, and on the mutual happiness which it has so much promoted, and the common renown which it has so greatly contributed to acquire." Here, he once again alluded to the fact that Hayne disparaged internal improvements but had asked for Webster's help in securing funds for a railroad in South Carolina.

Hayne's version of the Union meant no true union at all; instead, he described a loose confederation of sovereign and hopelessly self-interested states. The people's creation, the central government, had to be supreme over the states, lest the nation have "no constitution of general government, and are thrust back again to the days of the Confederation." The events of 1787, then, had redefined the nation, but Hayne seemed to desire a return to the chaos of the 1780s. Nullification promised more anarchy. How could a nation survive, Webster asked, if each of the twenty-four states possessed the power to decide which laws met constitutional muster? No, the people, not the states, had created the Union. "It is, Sir, the people's Constitution, the people's government, made for the people, made by the people, and answerable to the people."[52] And if the government they created became despotic, then they had the right to cast it off. Nullification, though, usurped the people's right of revolution by creating a perpetual revolution of a disgruntled minority. The national government, then, had the competency within its individual branches to determine and interpret the people's will, not a state legislature or a nullification convention.

Several times during Webster's speech, Hayne interjected to ask if his colleague sought to deny the right to revolution against a tyrannical government. Hayne sought to portray nullification as a more peaceful and less destructive form of resistance against tyranny, as if South Carolina did the Union a favor by engaging in resistance and not revolution. Webster would have nothing of Hayne's description of nullification as a peaceful mode of opposition. Yes, Webster conceded, the people had the right to cast off despotism. Nullification, however, perverted the very idea of majority government by giving the minority veto power over every form of legislation. And what, Webster asked, if South Carolina did nullify the tariff? Would not such an absurd policy negate the rights of other states that believed the law constitutional? If Hayne's true intent mirrored the Virginia and Kentucky Resolutions of 1798—an official remonstrance by a state against a federal law and a request for redress of grievances—then so be it. But of course Hayne and the nullifiers meant no such thing; instead, they sought to usurp majority rule by empowering a tyrannical minority. At the end of his address, Webster turned to Hayne for full effect. Webster did not care to even consider Hayne's vision of the Union, as he made clear in a stunning peroration:

I have not allowed myself, Sir, to look beyond the Union, to see what might lie hidden in the dark recess behind. I have not coolly weighed the chances of preserving liberty when the bonds that unite us together shall be broken asunder. I have not accustomed myself to hang over the precipice of disunion, to see whether, with my short sight, I can fathom the depth of the abyss below; nor could I regard him as a safe counsellor in the affairs of this government, whose thoughts should be mainly bent on considering, not how the Union may be best preserved, but how tolerable might be the condition of the people when it should be broken up and destroyed. While the Union lasts, we have high, exciting, gratifying prospects spread out before us and our children. Beyond that I seek not to penetrate the veil. God grant that in my day, at least, that curtain may not rise! God grant that on my vision never may be opened what lies behind! When my eyes shall be turned to behold for the last time the sun in heaven, may I not see him shining on the broken and dishonored fragments of a once glorious Union; on States dissevered, discordant, belligerent; on a land rent with civil feuds, or drenched, it may be, in fraternal blood! Let their last feeble and lingering glance rather behold the gorgeous ensign of the republic, now known and honored throughout the earth, still full high advanced, its arms and trophies streaming in their original lustre, not a stripe erased or polluted, not a single star obscured, bearing for its motto, no such miserable interrogatory as "What is all this worth?" nor those other words of delusion and folly, "Liberty first and Union afterwards"; but everywhere, spread all over in characters of living light, blazing on all it sample folds, as they float over the sea and over the land, and in every wind under the whole heavens, that other sentiment, dear to every true American heart,—Liberty *and* Union, now and for ever, one and inseparable!

Hayne made a brief reply to clarify a few points, but the debate for the day had ended with Webster's iconic words. The hushed audience had streamed from the hall, entranced by the speech. Webster took his chair, and a southern senator approached him to say, "Mr. Webster, I think you had better die now, and rest your fame on that speech." Hayne heard the remark and replied in a way that betrayed the good-natured side of the man, "You ought not to die: a man who can make such speeches as that ought never to die." Later that evening at a reception hosted by President Jackson, Hayne and Webster met again. "How are you to-night," Webster asked his debate partner. "None the better for you, sir," Hayne responded, with a touch of humor.[53]

Webster had carried the day—and the debate. In one speech, he had demolished the nullifiers and articulated a vision of nationalism that would challenge Americans' beliefs about the nature of their union for generations. The brilliance of his oratory had enraptured the Senate audience. It took a month for the nation to read the entire speech, as Webster made significant revisions to the text for publication. The original version as transcribed by veteran congressional reporter Joseph Gales could not possibly capture the presentation itself, with Webster's changes of inflection, his arm movements, his glances made for theatrical effect. But neither could the revision, in spite of Webster's best efforts. By the end of February, the revised speech headed to the printer. Gales and Seaton, publishers of the *Register of Debates* and the *National Intelligencer*, published forty thousand copies of the speech in pamphlet form; some twenty other editions brought Webster's words to as many as one hundred thousand more.

Webster had succeeded at giving voice to a conception of the Union that many Americans had not considered. Most Americans saw the United States as a plural rather than singular form. Their union was an experiment that might succeed or fail. The states themselves had predated the Union and might survive beyond its demise. Webster's speech marked an important effort in seeing the Union as perpetual and supreme. But Calhoun and Hayne would not relent in the face of a brilliant speech. Nullification still loomed over the nation.

5

Nullification and Nationhood

JACKSON HAD CLOSELY FOLLOWED the debate between Webster and Hayne, receiving reports from one of his confidants who monitored the deliberations from the Senate chamber. After the first day of Webster's second reply to Hayne, Jackson asked William Beverley Smith, one of his closest managers, to update him on the day's speechmaking.

"Been to the Capitol, Major?" asked Jackson.

"Yes, General."

"Well, and how is Webster getting on?"

"He is delivering a most powerful speech," Smith replied. "I am afraid he is demolishing our friend Hayne."

"I expected it," answered the president.[1]

Until the Webster-Hayne Debate, nullification had not loomed large in the mind of President Andrew Jackson, who considered the ideas emanating from South Carolina as mere saber rattling from an embattled minority determined to get its way. Jackson even sympathized with the aggrieved southerners on the tariff issue, believing that Congress needed to modify the Tariff of 1828 to restore balance and sectional harmony. The president, an ardent defender of states' rights, had warned Congress in his first annual message to resist "all encroachments upon the legitimate sphere of State sovereignty," namely the economic nationalism espoused by the heirs to Federalism—the National Republicans.[2] But the debate had awakened Jackson to the danger of Hayne's—and Calhoun's—extreme version of state sovereignty.

Jackson expected Webster to smash the nullifiers because he believed they had developed a perverted notion of states' rights. Daniel Webster and Andrew Jackson may have disagreed on many issues—maybe even most issues— but they agreed on one matter: the people had the right to rule. Just as the new president had admonished Congress to protect state sovereignty in his first annual message, so too did he state that "*The majority is to govern.*"[3] He wrote those words in the context of the election of 1824, where the people's choice for president, namely himself, had lost the presidency by a vote in the House of Representatives to John Quincy Adams. The will of the people had been thwarted. Nullification presented a similar situation; the will of the South Carolina nullifiers threatened to usurp the majority. Jackson soon recognized that he and his allies needed to counteract the radical ideology coming from the Palmetto State.[4] How Jackson, and the entire nation, would respond to the issues raised in Webster's and Hayne's speeches captured the attention of Washington and the nation in the early months of 1830, even as the debate continued within the Senate.

Just as the debate had transcended its initial purpose, the sale of western lands, so too did the debate in Congress descend from the heights of Webster's and Hayne's spirited forensics. The four speeches stood on their own as complete articulations of two different visions of union. Alas, the solons of the Senate could not keep their silence. Between January and May 1830, twenty-one of the forty-eight senators delivered a staggering sixty-five speeches on the nature of the Union. Most merely rehashed the points that Webster and Hayne had made in their addresses. As historian Merrill Peterson aptly described the proceedings, "The hawks had flown, but the buzzards descended to feast on the carrion."[5]

The debate led to a strange sort of catharsis by which the senators unleashed their grievances on a multitude of issues that related only peripherally to the original resolution on public lands. Webster had opened the debate to a discussion of the federal Union, and now senator after senator stormed into the breach to offer his own interpretation of the Constitution. The tenor of the debate strayed far from Webster's soaring vision of national unity as the senators laid bare the deep-seated sectional differences that existed within

President Andrew Jackson, pictured in his second term in office. All eyes turned to Jackson to see whether he sided with Hayne or Webster on the nature of the Union. His answer, memorably given at the Democratic Party's 1830 Jefferson Day dinner, surprised many of his southern supporters. Courtesy of the Library of Congress. Reproduction number LC-USZCN4-178

the Union. Careful observers might have even noticed the raw sectionalism in Webster's speech as he sought to defend New England from the memory of the Hartford Convention. Webster sought to articulate a new vision of the federal Union, but he crowned New England as the defender and exemplar of that tradition.[6] Webster's speech gave rhetorical form to the efforts of a generation of political leaders to implement political and economic nationalism in the United States, but even Webster could not resist the temptation to define American nationalism in sectional terms. Henry Clay's American System, for example, stood at the forefront of efforts to bind the nation together. The tariff, national banking, and internal improvements were tools that would accomplish the task of bringing the nation together. Yet any efforts at implementing the program became enmeshed in local and regional politics. The debate over national development invigorated sectionalism as different parts of the Union sought the advantage. "Instead of extinguishing sectionalism," one historian has noted, "the American System was breeding it."[7]

The endless speechifying deepened the sense of division within the Senate and, by extension, the Union. Some senators undoubtedly sought greater glory by hoping to reach the level of Webster's and Hayne's oratory, but no one proved equal to the task. Most, however, sought to vindicate their section, their people, against the claims and calumnies of others. That the debate lasted five months testifies to the wide-ranging opinions on what sort of nation their forefathers had created. The speeches had a common characteristic: virtually every one of them offered a specific version of history designed to uphold their claims regarding the issues under deliberation. Speaker after speaker sought to recall the true history of the founding in order to recover the true meaning of "We the People." Webster's and Hayne's extended discourse on who authored the Northwest Ordinance serves as but one example of how the senators filled their addresses with historical references designed to bolster their claims. Instead of proving one version correct over another, the senators revealed the contested history of the founding era. On several levels, consensus eluded the participants.

For his part, Thomas Hart Benton showed little interest in consensus. After Webster's final speech, the Missouri senator could not help but indulge his desire to refute the claims of his Bay State colleague. In a bitter, rambling speech, Benton lambasted Webster's invocation of disunion as alarmist and out of place in a sober discussion of public issues. True to his combative form, Benton said that there was a time "when such a speech would have found, in its delivery, every attribute of a just and rigorous propriety," namely "when the Hartford Convention was in session! when the language in the Capitol was 'Peaceably if we can, forcibly, if we must!'"[8] Most of the speech, however, reiterated Benton's earlier statements on the American System and his preferred policies for land distribution in the West.

Other senators addressed specific details of Webster's speech that concerned federal power, the role of the Supreme Court, the supremacy of federal law, and the idea of nullification. Benton's speech touched on these issues, but his discursive remarks did not home in on any specific issue in detail. Kentucky senator John Rowan spoke at length in favor of state sovereignty and interposition against overreaching federal power. Webster had argued that the people, not the states, formed the Union. The states, in acting as signatories to the Constitution had surrendered a portion, though not all, of their sovereignty. Rowan demurred, arguing that such an act amounted to the "voluntary dissolution of their social compacts" of the states themselves.[9] Nationalists like Webster, Rowan contended, sought to destroy state sovereignty by marginalizing the role of the states in building the Union and subjugating the states to federal law as interpreted by the Supreme Court. Rowan argued that "the sovereign power of a State is an unfit subject to be disposed of by judicial decision; and that the Supreme Court is an unfit tribunal to dispose of the sovereignty of the States."[10] Aligning himself to a degree with Hayne, Rowan insisted that in disputes involving a state's sovereignty, Congress must "refer the question to an infinitely more exalted tribunal than the Supreme Court. I mean to the States of this Union."[11] Here, Rowan followed the logic of the Virginia and Kentucky Resolutions of 1798, which Hayne claimed as the justification for his version of nullification as well.

For what purpose did the Supreme Court exist if not to act as the final arbiter of matters concerning constitutional interpretation? In his first major speech in the Senate, John M. Clayton of Delaware asked this very question. Elected to the Senate as a National Republican in 1828, Clayton largely supported Webster's arguments. "State sovereignty and State rights constitute the very war cry of a new party in this country," Clayton warned his colleagues.[12] The proponents of nullification had elevated the states to a level beyond the reach of the people themselves. The people created the states, Clayton argued, and they could take away or reassign any attributes of sovereignty as they saw fit. In ratifying the Constitution, the people of the states had done the latter by ceding certain powers to the newly created federal government.

More ominously, the nullifiers proposed an arrangement by which "one State is to govern all the rest, whenever she may choose to declare, by convention, that a law is unconstitutional."[13] A state convention, just like a citizen, had the right to pronounce a law as unconstitutional, but such a declaration amounted to the exercise of free speech and not a declaration that effectively bound the other states and would lead to disunion. "It comes at last, then, to this," Clayton reasoned, "that we have no other direct resource, in the cases we have been considering, to save us from the horrors of anarchy, than the Supreme Court of the United States."[14]

Clayton made one of the most compelling cases against nullification of any senator save Daniel Webster. He illustrated how the South Carolinians would create anarchy and threaten civil war by nullifying the tariff. Clayton, too, chastised his southern colleagues for threatening the integrity of the Union over money. In an incisive rhetorical flourish, Clayton stated that "whenever pounds, shillings, and pence, alone, shall be arrayed against the infinite blessings of the Union, I shall unhesitatingly prefer the latter, for the simple reason that I can never learn how to 'calculate its value.'"[15]

By the time Clayton finished his speech on March 4, 1830, dozens of senators had entered the seemingly interminable debate. Not a single speech so far had given the senators, or the people, much idea of what President Andrew Jackson thought of the proceedings. The closest indication we have of Jackson's opinions before he delivered his famous toast at the Jefferson Day banquet on April 13 came from a speech delivered by Louisiana senator Edward Livingston, an important Jackson ally and a leader of the Jacksonian forces in the Senate. A longtime friend of Old Hickory who would come to play a critical role in the nullification controversy, Livingston stood with Thomas Hart Benton and New Hampshire senator Levi Woodbury as the administration's spokesmen in the Senate. Livingston's speech stands out among the others as a learned attempt to find a middle ground between the positions that Webster and Hayne elucidated. Moreover, Livingston's speech illustrates a final element of what made the celebrated debate of 1830 so revelatory about political culture in the early republic. As "the official spokesman for the Administration," according to his biographer, the Louisiana senator's speech outlined the president's own thoughts on the nature of the Union and the menace of nullification.[16]

Livingston rejected both the ultranationalist vision of Webster and the extreme states' rights position of Hayne. To Webster, he responded that the states indeed had entered into a "compact of each one with the whole." To Hayne, he countered that that the people had acted through the states to surrender irrevocably a portion of their sovereignty to the federal government.

The people had, through the states, created the nation and had submitted themselves to its authority on specific matters, including the right of the Supreme Court to make judgment on issues of constitutional law.

Elaborating on themes he had previously developed during the heated discussion of internal improvements in the Eighteenth Congress, Livingston balanced the imperative of states' rights with nationalism by arguing that the Union had attributes of a consolidated *and* a federal union. "This government," Livingston concluded, "is neither such a federative one, founded on a compact, as leaves to all the parties their full sovereignty, nor such a consolidated popular government, as deprives them of the whole of that sovereign power." The founders, instead, had created a divided sovereignty in which the people had acted through the states to create and adopt the Constitution. The Constitution, in turn, provided for the method of dividing sovereignty between the states and the federal government. The senator believed in a far more nuanced compact theory of union than Hayne had considered. To Livingston's mind, the states and the people within them had entered into a compact in which each state ceded certain attributes of sovereignty to the national government. In keeping with the older states' rights tradition, Livingston argued that the individual states had the right to remonstrate to Congress, the Supreme Court, or the other states, against any federal exercise of power they deemed unconstitutional. These principles, and not the nullification doctrines of Hayne and Calhoun, were the true principles of 1798. And these principles largely reflected the opinions of President Andrew Jackson.[17]

Nullification, Livingston argued, did not reside in the powers reserved to the states. The introduction of Hayne and Calhoun's version of nullification into the government "would totally change its nature, make it inefficient, invite to dissension, and end, at no distant period, in separation." The senator claimed that the founders would have rejected any such proposal within the constitutional convention. So, too, would Jefferson and Madison have rejected it within the Virginia and Kentucky Resolutions. The resolutions, according to Livingston's interpretation, asserted the right of a state to issue a remonstrance against a law it deemed unconstitutional. Like John Clayton, Livingston concurred that the right to *protest* a law did not allow a state to nullify its operation within a state's boundaries. The states could "co-operate in procuring its repeal," but no state could unilaterally declare it null and void. Livingston anticipated the argument that Thomas Jefferson had asserted the right of a state to "nullify" an unconstitutional law, but he dismissed any notion that Jefferson had implied any action beyond Madison's conception of remonstrance. The ability to "arrest the execution of the law" within a state was, according to Livingston, "a more modern invention, and, as I think I have proved, utterly incompatible with the nature of our Government." The ultimate constitutional remedy, then, rested in the Supreme Court's judgment of a law's constitutionality or a constitutional amendment. Livingston did uphold the right of secession, but only as a last resort when the states had exhausted all other means to redress their grievances. He made clear, too, that secession could follow only in the extreme exercise of oppression—when the federal government had broken the constitutional compact and therefore absolved the states of their obligation to submit to the charter.

Livingston not only rejected the baneful doctrine of nullification, but he also lamented an "excess of party rage" that threatened mature deliberation and even national unity. As the debate wore on, some of the senators reflected on the influence of party politics in national politics. John Clayton had even alluded to the seeds of a southern states' rights party forming among the nullifiers and ultra–states' rights proponents. Reckless partisanship under the pretense of constitutional construction perverted the virtue of political parties and threatened to divide the nation into warring camps on the meaning of the Union itself. Livingston called for politicians and the people to lay aside their passions and appeal to reason. For the Louisiana senator—and for President Jackson—the wellspring of reason lay in the people. "Let the partisans on either side of the argument," Livingston concluded, "be assured that the people will not submit to consolidation, nor suffer disunion; and that their good sense will detect the fallacy of arguments which lead to either."[18]

Historians have largely forgotten Edward Livingston and his efforts to seek consensus during the Webster-Hayne Debate, an omission that would have confounded his contemporaries. After his speech, Livingston won plaudits from none other than James Madison, who praised his interpretation of the Kentucky and Virginia Resolutions and lauded his efforts to steer a middle course between Hayne and Webster. "You have succeeded better in your interpretation of the Virginia proceedings in 98–99 than those who have seen in them, a co-incidence with the Nullifying doctrine so called," Madison wrote to Livingston. "This doctrine as new to me as it was to you, derives no support from the best contemporary elucidations of those proceedings."[19] Of course, Madison had his own legacy to preserve, and the words of Robert Hayne and his contention that the South Carolinians found their inspiration in the actions of Jefferson and Madison in 1798 and 1799 forced the surviving member of the duo to respond. Hayne forced the retired president's hand directly. Desirous of Madison's praise—and expecting that he would receive it—Hayne sent a copy of the speech to Madison, hoping for a letter of endorsement. The "spirit of '98" had become something of a rallying cry among the nullifiers, and to have the imprimatur of the author of the Virginia Resolutions, not to mention the Constitution, would have given credibility to Hayne and his allies. Madison, then, faced a dilemma. He had to disavow nullification, but in doing so he could not wholeheartedly endorse what he considered the boundless nationalism of Daniel Webster. Careful to absolve himself of any influence on the South Carolinians and eager to defend the Jeffersonian tradition of states' rights against the extreme designs of nullification, Madison responded with a four-thousand-word rebuttal of the "doctrines espoused in [Hayne's speeches] from which I am constrained to dissent."[20]

From Montpelier, Madison anguished over his response to the Webster-Hayne Debate. From the White House, Andrew Jackson calculated his next step. Livingston's speech offered at least a glimpse at where the president stood on the issues, but pressure intensified for Jackson to express his thoughts in his own words. That Duff Green, editor of the *U.S. Telegraph*, the mouthpiece of Old Hickory's administration, had published a series of editorials suggesting that Jackson supported the sentiments of Hayne and the nullifiers only intensified the pressure for the president to address the issue in his own words. The opportunity came on April 13, 1830, when Jacksonian luminaries held their annual celebration of Thomas Jefferson's birthday. Jackson had accepted an invitation to the dinner, as had Calhoun and Hayne. Jackson's secretary of state and increasingly influential political confidant Martin Van Buren alerted the president to his belief that Hayne and Calhoun might use the festivities to build support for their ideas on nullification and urged him to respond with "the utmost prudence and circumspection."[21] As president, Jackson felt certain that the organizers would ask him to deliver a toast. Here Jackson planned to deliver his response to Robert Hayne and John C. Calhoun.

In his office on the morning of April 13, Jackson penned three statements that he could deliver as the evening's toast and shared them with two associates. Both agreed that the briefest toast best reflected the president's own beliefs. The president pocketed the brief remarks and burned the other two pieces of paper. That evening, Jackson and the cabinet arrived at the Indian

Queen Hotel, located ten blocks up Pennsylvania Avenue from the White House. The president conferred with Van Buren on how to proceed with the evening's plans. "Thus armed," Van Buren recollected in his autobiography, "we repaired to the dinner with feelings on the part of the old Chief akin to those which would have animated his breast if the scene of this preliminary skirmish in defence of the Union had been the field of battle instead of the festive board."[22]

The guests celebrated lustily, making twenty-four toasts to the great principles of the Jeffersonian tradition that Jackson and his advisors had resurrected. Most of them lauded the states' rights heritage of American politics as embodied in the Virginia and Kentucky Resolutions. Then came Robert Hayne, who had organized the event, with his ardent defense of his version of the spirit of 1798. He concluded with the words "The *Union* of the States, and the *Sovereignty* of the States."[23] By the time Hayne completed his speech and toast, the president had started to lose patience with the remarks offered, some of which he considered seditious and completely against the principles of Thomas Jefferson. Jackson wrote his own toast on the back of the list of toastmasters and prepared to stand. But in writing, he omitted a single word. He stood, turned toward John C. Calhoun, seated close by, and uttered "Our Union: *It must be preserved.*"[24]

"The veil was rent—the incantations of the night were exposed to the light of day," Van Buren recalled years later.[25] The diminutive secretary of state, who perched himself upon a chair to see the moment, recalled the effect of the words. Hayne rushed to the president and asked him to add the word "federal" to blunt the effect of the brief riposte. Jackson "cheerfully assented" as he had mistakenly omitted the word.[26] An additional word could not temper the president's toast. Jackson's reply to Hayne took only seven words, where Webster had delivered an entire speech. But both men agreed: the Union was supreme over the states. John C. Calhoun rose next, startled by Jackson's forceful declaration, and gamely offered his own toast to the Union: "The Union—next to our liberty the most dear; may we all remember that it can only be preserved by respecting the rights of the States and distributing equally the benefit and burden of the Union."[27] Ever the political operator, Van Buren rose in an attempt to smooth the argument that had erupted in the open. "Mutual forbearance and reciprocal concession; thro' their agency the Union was established. The patriotic spirit from which they emanated will forever sustain it."[28] Union had become the focal point in all the speechifying and toast making. No one could mistake that Andrew Jackson supported the Union as supreme.[29]

Jackson left the dinner at ten o'clock, grousing that the designing politicians had reduced the festivities to "a piece of political management."[30] Yet Jackson himself had practiced politics artfully for the occasion. Jackson felt manipulated by some of his closest associates, including Calhoun and Duff Green, who had tried their best to turn the evening's celebration into a nullification affair. Jackson's relationship with his vice president, already strained by other issues, withered after the Jefferson dinner. Green alienated himself from the president by his own machinations. Jackson, a stubborn man to say the least, deepened in his resolve to resist nullification and the perverted efforts of the nullifiers who dared calculate the value of the Union. That the president's stance had become rigid became clearer just a few days after the Jefferson dinner, when a South Carolina congressman came to visit Jackson at the White House. Jackson greeted the congressman cordially, but the conversation turned when the visitor asked if Jackson had a message for his associates in the Palmetto State. "No, I believe not," the president replied initially, but then he amended his statement. "Yes, I have; please give my compliments to my friends in your State, and say to them, that if a single drop of blood shall be shed there in opposition to the laws of the United States, I will hang the first man I can lay my hand on engaged in such treasonable conduct, upon the first tree I can reach." Startled, the guest made a fast exit.[31]

Jackson's intemperate remarks to the South Carolina congressman illustrated the president's belief that the nullifiers proposed a course of action that could indeed lead to civil war and bloodshed. Edward Livingston's remarks on the effect of nullification had indeed represented Jackson's own beliefs. Hayne, Calhoun, and the nullifiers portrayed their brainchild as a savior of the Union; Jackson, Livingston, and their allies saw it as the death knell for the Union. But focusing on Jackson's denunciation of nullification without looking at his opinions on the root cause of the nullifiers' campaign obscures the contradictory impulses that the president faced in charting his course. Jackson had supported elements of the American System, especially the tariff, much to the consternation of some of his southern colleagues. "It is time we should become a little more *Americanized*," Jackson wrote to a southern colleague in 1824, "and instead of feeding the paupers and laborers of Europe, feed our own, or else in a short time, by continuing our present policy, we shall all be paupers ourselves."[32] To Jackson's mind, the tariff could accomplish the aims of reducing the nation's debt, promoting national development, and strengthening America's position against European powers. Four years of John Quincy Adams's economic program, however, convinced Jackson that the tariff could promote inequality instead of prosperity. Government, according to Jackson, had no right to pick winners and losers. "If [government] would confine itself to equal protection," Jackson wrote in his June 1832 veto of the bill rechartering the Bank of the United States, "and, as Heaven does its rains, shower its favors alike on the high and low, the rich and the poor, it would be an unqualified blessing."[33] The American System, in the hands of Henry Clay and Adams, blessed some at the expense of others.

By the time he ascended to the presidency, then, Jackson bore a healthy skepticism toward the American System. His veto of the Maysville Road bill in May 1830 illustrated his belief that private ventures should not rely on public capital, especially when the benefits of a project resided in one state or in one region. The veto, and its accompanying message, had other purposes. Secretary of State Martin Van Buren, whose star was fast rising in Jackson's circle of political confidants, encouraged the president to issue the veto with a message upholding states' rights as a way of isolating South Carolina's nullifiers from the more mainstream southern opinion. Though he came out against internal improvements, Jackson continued to hold a more favorable view of tariffs. The nullification crisis, however, challenged his beliefs. As much as Jackson blustered and threatened the South Carolina nullifiers, he recognized too that a gradual reduction in the tariff might assuage their concerns and thereby defuse the situation. With the treasury running a surplus by 1831, it only became easier to propose a reduction in the tariff rates. Eventually, Jackson's desire for sectional concord trumped his concerns about national economic development.

Jackson's response to the nullification crisis revolved around both practical and theoretical considerations. In practical terms, Jackson faced the difficult position of trying to forge a compromise between northerners and southerners on the tariff, the purported catalyst that sparked the crisis itself. Tariff reform provided the peaceful means to escape the crisis. On the one hand, Jackson had to convince commercial interests in the North to accept reduced tariffs in order to placate southern concerns. On the other hand, he had to convince southerners that they could and should accept a less burdensome form of protection. Neither task would prove easy. Northern manufacturers coveted protectionism and resented the nullifiers' efforts to hold the Union hostage over economic concerns. Southerners seemed dangerously united against what they considered oppressive taxation. Could the Palmetto State radicalism spread beyond the state's borders? To Jackson, it seemed a distinct possibility. Virginia's governor lent a sympathetic ear to the nullifiers, and other states had indicated a willingness to consider South Carolina's plans.

Theoretical considerations also complicated Jackson's efforts to secure peace while stamping out nullification. The Webster-Hayne Debate, in its entirety, had shown that three schools of thought existed among Americans attempting to answer the question of whether the American republic was a confederation of small republics or was a larger national republic itself. Hayne, Webster, and Livingston had represented each school. One bloc, represented by Hayne, viewed the nation as a confederation of small republics united for specific purposes. Each republic within the confederation, however, retained its sovereignty. A second bloc, represented by Webster, claimed that the Union was a republic itself, created by the people, and ultimately sovereign over the states. Livingston represented the third bloc, which believed that the people, through the states, had divided sovereignty between the states and the national republic. These federals, nationals, and centrists, as one historian of nullification has termed them, each held a different conception of the Union. Armed with different versions of American history, the proponents of each conception of union sought to assert their position during the Webster-Hayne Debate and thereafter as the United States headed toward a constitutional crisis over nullification.[34]

Jackson and the Congress moved forward on the plan to moderate the tariff rates of 1828 in an effort to neutralize the nullifiers and forestall the spread of nullification beyond South Carolina. The Tariff of 1832 lowered duties from their 1828 levels, but local politics got in the way of more substantial reform. Manufacturers in the Northeast successfully lobbied their congressmen to maintain rates on a number of items precious to their interests. By the time Jackson received the final product, the Tariff of 1832 legislation did little to address the grievances of South Carolina, which seemed more resolute than ever to resist protectionism and the federal government. The rhetoric of nullification, combined with the fevered response of South Carolinians to the August 1831 slave revolt of Nat Turner in Southampton County, Virginia, had convinced the nullifiers that the Northeast intended to subjugate the South and threaten its peculiar institution. In their feverish state of mind, the nullifiers had linked the tariff with abolitionism as twin northern plots to destroy the southern way of life. Calhoun's "Fort Hill address," which he issued just before word reached South Carolina about the Nat Turner revolt, laid bare Calhoun's concern that the South had grown weak in the face of northern industrialization. In the end, his fears overcame his hopes for progress. Though intrigued by and even supportive of progress, Calhoun feared for the loss of the agrarian way of life that southerners enjoyed, and, of course, was provided by enslaved labor. Though he avoided the word, the Fort Hill address endorsed nullification. Daniel Webster called the address "the ablest and most plausible, and therefore the most dangerous vindication of that particular form of Revolution which has yet appeared."[35]

Armed with almost four years' defense of nullification, South Carolina forged ahead with its plans to resist federal law. Appeasement, via a revised tariff schedule, had failed to quiet the radicals. By the fall of 1832, South Carolina seemed poised to nullify the tariff. A special session of the state legislature met in October to authorize a nullification convention to meet the following month. The nullifiers and unionists fought bitterly throughout the fall of 1832 over the nullification issue, but with a two-thirds majority in the South Carolina legislature the nullifiers had complete control of the situation. Unionists pleaded for caution but to no avail as the nullifiers seized control of the convention by electing their slate of delegates. The planter elite in the Palmetto State held the levers of power, and the majority of them wanted a confrontation with Jackson and the federal government. On November 24, 1832, the nullification convention declared the tariff "null, void, and of no law" within South Carolina and prohibited the collection of duties within the state.[36]

Robert Hayne and John C. Calhoun feared, with good reason, the forces they had unleashed. By the time the convention adopted its ordinance nullifying the tariff, divisions had emerged among the nullifiers themselves. Conservatives and radicals fought over the ultimate outcome of South Carolina's crusade. Key northern politicians, like Daniel Webster, had predicted that the hotspurs in South Carolina saw nullification as a first step toward the creation of a southern confederacy. The radical wing of the nullifiers seemed to confirm their beliefs when they demanded the immediate enforcement of nullification. A compromise emerged when February 1, 1833, emerged as the day on which South Carolina would enforce nullification if the federal government did not act to suspend the tariff and acquiesce to the state's terms. At the same time, the state's coterie of leaders shuffled the key positions of power. Robert Hayne would resign from his Senate seat to replace the outgoing governor, James Hamilton. Calhoun, who stood to lose his job in a few months, resigned the vice presidency to take Hayne's place in the Senate. Hayne would assume the task of making sure that nullification went to plan, that no hotheads would spoil the process and jeopardize the much-sought-after support of the other southern states. Freed from the vice presidential chair above the Senate chamber's dais, Calhoun would advocate for the Palmetto State's interests and against Daniel Webster's new nationalism from the Senate floor.

Hayne's inaugural address as governor of South Carolina show how completely the Calhounites had repudiated the American nationalism they had endorsed after the War of 1812. "The speedy establishment, on the ruins of the rights of the states, and the liberties of the people, of a great CONSOLIDATED GOVERNMENT," threatened the founders' intent for the Union, according to Hayne. Quoting Jefferson, Hayne accused nationalists like Webster of "'riding and ruling over the plundered ploughman and beggared yeomanry' of our once happy land—our glorious confederacy, broken into scattered and dishonored fragments—the light of liberty extinguished, never perhaps to be resumed." The nullifiers, he argued, "struggled gloriously to avert" the dissolution of the Union but, in the end, had to stand for their own rights. The nationalists, in Hayne's logic, forced South Carolina and her allies to disunion.[37]

\Excitement soon faded as it became clear that South Carolina had moved precipitously toward nullification and disunion, outpacing public opinion in the other southern states. Most of the other southern states despised the tariff, too, but their attachment to the Union precluded cooperation with nullification. The legislatures of Alabama, Georgia, and Mississippi repudiated nullification in strong terms; other southern legislatures followed suit. Georgia called for a southern convention to debate the tariff, but its legislature could not support the "rash and revolutionary" policy undertaken by the nullifiers.[38]

President Jackson, who with Martin Van Buren as his vice presidential candidate, had won the popular vote for the presidency, now had to respond. On December 4, Jackson transmitted his annual message to Congress, a document that seemed to offer South Carolina an olive branch. Jackson indicated his opposition to nullification but made clear that he believed tariff reform the only sensible way to defuse the crisis. Moreover, Jackson gave a ringing defense of states' rights. For a man who had threatened to hang the nullifiers, the speech seemed remarkably conciliatory. What followed, however, satis-

"An epitaph for the Union." An 1832 antinullification broadside from Philadelphia arguing that if nullifiers like Robert Hayne, who was by now governor of South Carolina, got their way, the Union would be destroyed. Courtesy of the Library of Congress. Reproduction number LC-USZ62-42778

fied even the most ardent nationalists, who considered Andrew Jackson an enemy to their cause. Six days later, Jackson issued his Nullification Proclamation, which left no doubt as to where the president stood on South Carolina and the nullification menace.

In drafting important state papers, Jackson usually consulted his Kitchen Cabinet of informal advisors. Amos Kendall, editor of the *Washington Globe*, produced an initial draft for the president to consider, but Jackson jettisoned the effort as too conciliatory. Jackson needed a document that differed markedly from his annual message, which sought to pacify South Carolina. The proclamation had to have the force of Jackson's will behind it while respecting his views on states' rights and the nature of the Union. Jackson turned to

Secretary of State Edward Livingston for assistance with the document. Jackson assigned Livingston the task for two reasons. First, Livingston's speech during the Webster-Hayne Debate closely followed Jackson's own beliefs on states' rights and the Union. Second, Livingston's speech had won praise from James Madison, who believed that the Louisiana senator's remarks captured the meaning behind Madison and Jefferson's words written some thirty-two years earlier. Jackson's cabinet had suggested that he consult with the retired president on how to explain why nullification deviated from the spirit of 1798. Though no evidence exists suggesting that Livingston and Jackson consulted Madison directly on the Nullification Proclamation, they did follow the line of argument that the sage of Montpelier had endorsed three years earlier in Livingston's contribution to the Webster-Hayne Debate.[39]

Jackson penned the first draft, hurriedly scratching out the words he wished to use in order to defend the Union, his own definition of states' rights, and how the nullifiers threatened both. Jackson handed the draft over to Livingston, lodged at the Decatur House across Lafayette Square from the White House. The secretary of state pored over the draft and the accompanying notes for three or four days before returning them to the president. When Jackson received the edited draft, he expressed disappointment. Livingston had not captured the essence of what Jackson wanted to say. Jackson, who valued the people as the fount of good government, wanted to express his belief that the people must support him in this crusade against treason and disunion. Livingston had missed the point. Meanwhile, Jackson continued work himself. At 11:00 p.m. on December 4, Jackson scribbled a conclusion that he felt would explain why Americans must stand against nullification. Finally, on Friday afternoon, Livingston returned with the final draft. Jackson expressed his satisfaction with Livingston's revisions and, aside from a few minor revisions of his own, ordered the text printed for distribution.

The document bears the thoughtful constitutional logic of Livingston's 1830 speech on the nature of the Union while exhibiting the forceful presence of Andrew Jackson's personality. Nullification subverted the Constitution and presaged the destruction of the Union. Loyal Americans must denounce it, according to Jackson, because nullification was "incompatible with the existence of the Union, contradicted expressly by the letter of the Constitution, unauthorized by its spirit, inconsistent with very principle on which it was founded, and destructive of the great object for which it was formed."[40] Following Livingston's argument from 1830, Jackson stated that the people, acting through the states, had created the Constitution, a document that "forms a *government*, not a league."[41] The president did not represent the states but the people.

A state had two means of redress when it believed that Congress had over-stepped its boundaries: it could appeal to the Supreme Court or to the people via the states acting in a constitutional convention. Nullification subverted the will of the people by allowing the states to interpret the law and by threat-ening disunion should they not get their way. In both cases, nullification al-lowed states to assume powers they did not possess. As Jackson's foremost biographer states, "Again and again he stated his fundamental decree: The people are sovereign. The Union is perpetual."[42]

Jackson concluded the proclamation with a direct appeal to the citizens of South Carolina, imploring them to consider the blessings of the Union and the perils of destroying what the people had created. Here Jackson sought to define what he called "the proud title of *American citizen*" in an era when na-tional citizenship seemed nebulous at best. The Union had produced count-less benefits for its citizens and had brought safety and stability to all the states, all the people. "Behold it as the asylum where the wretched and the oppressed find a refuge and support," Jackson wrote. "Look on this picture of happiness and honor and say, *We too are citizens of America*."[43] South Carolina could not succeed in its efforts to nullify federal law and destroy the Union. The other states would not support its revolutionary venture, and the federal government would use force if necessary to stop the drift toward dissolution of the Union.

Jackson's twin December messages, the annual message to Congress and the Nullification Proclamation, served dual purposes not unlike a carrot and stick approach. The annual message sought to reassure states' rights propo-nents, while the proclamation sought to end the specter of nullification and disunion. Jackson had to show wary southerners that he did not support the ultranationalism of Daniel Webster. At the same time, however, he had to as-suage northerners that Hayne, Calhoun, and the nullifiers espoused a version of states' rights far outside of mainstream constitutional thought. Livingston had paved the way in 1830 with his speech during the Webster-Hayne Debate; his work on the Nullification Proclamation finished the project by defining a centrist position of divided sovereignty. In Andrew Jackson's mind, divided sovereignty tempered both extremes on the spectrum of the nature of the Union. More pragmatically, the twin messages offered an exit strategy for the South Carolinians and for Jackson, who had threatened force against the

Palmetto State. The proclamation reinforced that Jackson would use force against South Carolina if necessary, but the annual message made clear that Jackson was willing to compromise on the tariff issue.

Both sides hinted at compromise on duties. In his report accompanying the Ordinance of Nullification, Hayne had proposed a reduced tariff rate that would satisfy South Carolina, a far cry from the no-tariff stance of the most hotheaded nullifiers. Jackson had moved toward compromise, too, for he had earlier endorsed tariffs as a means of retiring the national debt and protecting certain industries. By December 1832, however, he seemed less concerned about those objectives and had begun calling for a reduction in duties that would placate southern free traders. A New York representative, Gulian C. Verplanck, proposed legislation to reduce the tariff over a period of two years to the levels of 1816. Jackson purportedly supported the Verplanck bill, but the effort bore Van Buren's fingerprints. Verplanck was an ally of the incoming vice president, which made it all but impossible for Calhoun to accept the olive branch. Protectionists in the North sought to sabotage the effort as well, predicting that the reduction would result in certain bankruptcy for manufacturers who could not possibly adjust to the lower rates in a two-year span.

In the short term, compromise seemed less certain as South Carolina moved toward nullification of the tariff. Jackson responded in kind, sending to Congress a request for legislation that would allow him to uphold federal law in the Palmetto State. The Force Bill provoked another debate within the Senate over nullification, with Daniel Webster and John C. Calhoun squaring off on the meaning of the Union. This time, however, events in South Carolina had transformed the discussion from a hypothetical discussion of constitutional law into an argument over a tangible crisis. Calhoun's resignation as vice president and his election to the Senate gave Webster what he had hoped for: an opportunity to debate the father of nullification. Though Webster and Jackson had been political foes on numerous occasions, they stood in lockstep on nullification. Webster endorsed the Force Bill, stating that "the President could not do otherwise than to recommend it to the consideration of Congress. He is not at liberty to look on and be silent, while dangers threatened the Union."[44]

Calhoun and Webster prepared for battle on the Senate floor over the Force Bill. South Carolina's new senator challenged the president's authority to use force against a sovereign state. Responding to Webster, Livingston, and Jackson, Calhoun concisely summarized his argument against the nationalists, among whom he now numbered the president: "I go on the ground that this constitution was made by the States; that it is a federal union of the States, in which the several States still retain their sovereignty." The Force Bill, in contrast, treated the states as vassals of the federal government. Calhoun talked of divided sovereignty, but he made clear his belief that the states reserved the bulk of their original powers. That the president believed that he could preserve the Union through federal authority only heightened the folly of his course. "You cannot keep the States united in their constitutional and federal bonds by force," Calhoun argued.[45] Finally, Calhoun turned to his more recent theories on majority rule. Further revealing his fears that the South was becoming a minority section in a Union dominated by northeastern commercial interests, he stated that the Union could survive only if the majority ceased oppressing the minority via unfair policies that extracted wealth from one section to benefit another. By reiterating his argument against nationalism and the American System, Calhoun only reinforced the belief that the nullifiers were calculating the value of the Union for their own economic benefits and with no eye toward the less tangible blessings of the nation.

Webster responded immediately, but he must have felt the pressure to at least equal, if not best, his second reply to Hayne. Calhoun was a different debate partner, however, in that he argued with less passion and more intellect. Webster would have to adjust to the difference, and he did. At the outset, Webster echoed Jackson's sentiments in the Nullification Proclamation that Calhoun's doctrine found support neither in the Constitution nor the people. Here again, Webster placed the people as the primary force behind the Union in a way that made Calhoun's insistence on state supremacy seem retrograde. He focused on two key points that underpinned Calhoun's theories on nullification. Calhoun believed that the states had formed the Union in compact and therefore had the right to determine the proper interpretation of the Constitution. Webster assailed both points by offering his own definition of the federal Union. Through the Constitution, the people created a government independent of and supreme over the states. No state could dissolve the Union without invoking the right of revolution. South Carolina's grievances did not meet that standard. The Constitution vested lawmaking authority in Congress, the execution of the laws in the president, and the interpretation of the laws in the judiciary. Nullification usurped federal power by allowing a single state to assume the role of the Supreme Court or a constitutional convention.

In sum, Webster defined the Union as one and inseparable. "The people of the United States," he explained, "are one people. They are one in making war, and one in making peace; they are one in regulating commerce, and one in laying duties of imposts. The very end and purpose of the Constitution was, to make them one people in these particulars; and it has effectually accomplished that object."[46] Through nullification and his theories on concurrent majorities, Calhoun sought to separate the people who created the Union into small and petty factions. Answering Calhoun's charge that a northern majority sought to subjugate the southern minority, Webster replied bluntly, "The majority *must* govern. In matters of common concern, the judgment of a majority *must* stand as the judgment of the whole."[47]

Finally, Webster sought to rally his audience by predicting that enough people in South Carolina believed in the Union that they would rally to its defense against the nullifiers and their program to thwart the will of the majority. Clearly seeking to match his brilliant 1830 peroration, Webster concluded with a stirring statement of his will to protect the Union: "I shall exert every faculty I possess in aiding to prevent the Constitution from being nullified, destroyed, or impaired; and even should I see it fall, I will still, with a voice feeble, perhaps, but earnest as ever issued from human lips, and with fidelity and zeal which nothing shall extinguish, call on the PEOPLE to come to its rescue."[48]

The Senate chamber erupted in cheers for Daniel Webster, "Defender of the Constitution."[49] Webster had linked arms across the political divide with President Jackson in defense of the Union and the will of the majority, expressed through the people themselves. For his part, Jackson believed that Webster had "demolished" Calhoun. "Mr. Webster handled him as a child," the president wrote to a South Carolina Unionist.[50] The debate between Webster and Calhoun encapsulated Congress's deliberations over the Force Bill. The vote in the Senate, which came on February 20, was a rout for the nullifiers, who exited the room as the yeas overwhelmed the opposition. Thirty-two senators voted in favor and one against—John Tyler of Virginia, who opposed nullification but also opposed the use of force against a state. The House of Representatives approved the bill on March 1, and Jackson signed it into law the following day.

The Force Bill kept up the pressure on South Carolina to back down from its position, which looked increasingly untenable as the days wore on. True, both the federal government and the state had commenced preparations to

deploy military forces, but conditions began to change amid the saber rattling. By March 1833, the nullifiers stood alone in the southern states. Facing
political isolation, the more moderate nullifiers like Robert Hayne began to
look for a means to achieve compromise. The state's leaders had already made
an important overture toward conciliation; on January 21, 1833, the legislature had voted to suspend the implementation of nullification until Congress
had the opportunity to debate a new round of tariff revisions. For a time, it
seemed as if Calhoun and Hayne had lost control of the movement they had
helped to spawn, but the early months of 1833 showed them reasserting their
power over the fractious radicals in the Palmetto State.

While Hayne sought to channel the radical spirit in his home state, Calhoun made efforts to craft a compromise in Washington. With the moribund
Verplanck tariff bill out of the way, Henry Clay emerged as a leader for compromise. Soon after Calhoun took his seat in the Senate, he joined forces
with Clay to draft a tariff bill that would satisfy southerners without drawing
the ire of the North. The alliance worked as both men, implacable foes of the
president, sought to create a compromise that Jackson had nothing to do with
but that he would have to accept. Over ten years, the legislation would lower
tariffs to approximately the levels in the Tariff of 1816. After 1842, the tariff
would remain only to produce the necessary revenue for government operations. Calhoun saw the final measure as a win for the opponents of protection, while manufacturers could claim—for a decade at least—that they had
retained protection for emerging industries. "The formula traded *time*," one
historian has observed, "of first importance to manufacturers, for *principle*, of
first importance to the South.[51]

Clay's plan, however, faced strong headwinds in Congress and at the White
House. The Clay plan split the National Republicans; westerners offered their
support, but easterners like Webster and John Quincy Adams opposed the
effort because it sacrificed the principle of protection. The Clay-Calhoun
project received a rebuke from Webster, who stated, "It is understood that
Mr. C[lay] will agree to almost any thing, in order to save the question, save
the Nullifiers & obtain the credit of *pacification*."[52] Certain Democrats likewise opposed the compromise tariff, if for no other reason than they wanted
Martin Van Buren, and not Henry Clay, to receive the credit for brokering
the compromise that saved the Union. Some worried about an alliance between the Kentuckian and South Carolinian and what it might mean for the
Jacksonian coalition. Others believed that the effort damaged the president's

reputation since he had not endorsed the Clay-Calhoun plan himself and had expressed his belief that the Force Bill needlessly provoked the South. Indeed, Clay encouraged opposition to Jackson's requests until it became clear that he would have to gain the president's support in order to pass the tariff reductions. In turn, Jackson eventually realized that he had to drop his own opposition to the Clay plan in the face of growing opposition within his own party. By February, Jackson had quieted his own belligerent rhetoric against the nullifiers and made clear to leaders on Capitol Hill that he would acquiesce in the tariff plan. In sum, political calculations played a significant role in reaction to and the passage of the compromise tariff.[53]

The Compromise of 1833 gave something to everyone. Southerners could boast that they had struck a blow against protectionism. Northerners had delayed the blow for a decade, however. For the West, legislation emerged to distribute public land revenues to the states, though Jackson would pocket-veto the bill. But when one looks at the balance sheet of who compromised on what, it becomes clear that Calhoun and the nullifiers gave much in their efforts to have peace. The South Carolinians had fallen into a trap of their own making with their belligerence and threats of disunion. As long as they believed that other southern states would rally to their side, those who donned the blue cockade in favor of nullification maintained their defiance. When the South made clear that it would not abandon the Union, the nullifiers had to back down.

First came the sword and then the olive branch. Several hours after it passed the Force Bill, the Senate voted in favor of the compromise tariff. Calhoun quickly left the capital for Columbia, where he informed the hotspurs that compromise had succeeded. Faced with isolation on the one hand and a viable alternative on the other, the radicals folded. Seeking to save face among their constituents, the radicals called another meeting of the nullification convention, where they defiantly nullified the Force Bill.

The Compromise of 1833, however, followed a troubling pattern that plagued several of the important settlements of the early American republic. As the historian Merrill Peterson has observed, the 1833 compromise prevailed in spite of the fact that no majority existed for the whole package. The Great Compromiser Henry Clay secured passage of the legislation only by breaking it into its different parts and calling for separate votes. Those congressmen who voted for the revised tariff tended to vote against the Force Bill. Of the 188 representatives who cast votes for the tariff and the Force Bill, 114 voted against one and for the other. Forty-three voted for the tariff and against the Force Bill; seventy-one voted vice versa.[54] Accordingly, one can argue that the so-called compromise may have staved off nullification, but it did little if anything to resolve the underlying issues that led to the crisis.

As for President Jackson, he could claim victory over the nullifiers though only with crucial assists from two of his greatest political foes, Daniel Webster and Henry Clay. Jackson paid a price for his efforts, however. Every time Jackson spoke of nationalism and federal union, he jeopardized Democratic support in the South. Wary southerners saw much to fear in an expansive definition of federal authority. For a time, they deflected blame toward Edward Livingston, whom they characterized as the real author of the Nullification Proclamation and the force behind Jackson's ardent defenses of national union. Yet they failed to recognize—or perhaps they did—that Jackson had taken those words as his own. Jackson lost much of his states' rights credibility with the southern wing of his party, which led to a number of southern politicians seeking to square the Jacksonian creed with their version of states' rights and Jeffersonian republicanism. The ever-present fear of interference with slavery left southerners wary of Jackson's muscular nationalism. For Jackson's part, the nullification crisis showed that even though Jackson owned slaves himself, he would not treat the institution as sacrosanct against threats to the Union.

Yet one must not overemphasize the rift; the coalition that Martin Van Buren had proposed to Thomas Ritchie years earlier remained. Many of those southerners who emerged from the nullification crisis with a mistrust of Andrew Jackson never supported him in the first place. Their misgivings regarding Old Hickory and their fears for the future of the South had existed in 1828 and had only heightened over the intervening four years. They were the elites who feared the loss of their power and influence amid the expansion of the white man's democracy and northern antipathy toward slavery. A second group of southerners, however, supported the president and his efforts to make government more responsive to the people's will. The South's yeoman farmers and small producers may have paused at his defense of nationalism during the crisis, but they had supported him in 1828 because Jackson supported states' rights and local government far more than the National Republicans did.

Jacksonian Democracy had emerged during the turbulent 1820s in many ways as a continuation of the age-old debate between the federalists and democrats, as Hayne labeled them in his second speech in the Senate. Indeed, Hayne, Webster, and their colleagues spoke at a time in which America's political culture was rapidly evolving toward a reoriented party structure in which the differences of old would become the points of contention in the present—all by design. Many of the speakers during the Webster-Hayne Debate, and indeed many citizens of the early American republic, believed that Americans had always been divided into two great parties. Whereas Webster called himself a National Republican, Hayne referred to himself as part of the "democrats of '98."[55] Their speechmaking, and the interminable discussion that followed in the spring of 1830 and even up to March 1833, suggested that Americans had always been arrayed in two great parties: one dedicated to strict construction of the Constitution, the other to a more expansive vision of national authority. In reality, regional differences, local customs, and differing economies suggested that American politics followed a far more complicated arrangement. To a considerable extent, Edward Livingston's 1830 speech and his efforts in composing the Nullification Proclamation over two years later revealed that the debate on the nature of the Union followed more along the lines of a continuum between ardent nationalism and states' rights. Livingston sought a middle ground between the two extreme positions of ultra–states' rights and nationalism that more accurately embodied the Jacksonian approach to the issue of constitutional construction. The debate over western lands, the tariff, and states' rights versus nationalism that had raged since Samuel Foot introduced his resolution on public lands in December 1829 forced Americans to confront the issue of how they defined the Union. Nationalists had once again articulated a vision of Union that had gone dormant since the end of the Era of Good Feelings, but the rapprochement negotiated in 1833 undermined the American System and left economic and political nationalists uncertain of their future. The Whig Party, which would emerge shortly, took up elements of their cause, but nothing had been settled. Likewise, the believers in states' rights faced a dilemma: Did they believe in perpetual union and majority or did they seek the protection of minority interests and the right of secession? The question, like so many others, remained unanswered.

Jackson's ascent to the presidency marked the beginning of a two-party system of American politics that sought to channel the issues discussed during the debate such as the tariff, internal improvements, western land policy, among others into a constructive political discourse among the people and their elected representatives. It sought to minimize the corrosive effect of slavery on the American body politic by forcing other issues to the forefront. And at the same time, the system sought to articulate and mediate competing visions of union in a country beset by intractable sectional divisions. Through the issues addressed in the Webster-Hayne Debate as well as the three visions of Union articulated by Webster, Hayne, and Livingston, we can see how Americans grappled with the problem of governance in the early American republic. We can also see foreshadowing of how they failed to contain the more destructive elements of their political discourse.[56]

The Webster-Hayne Debate in Historical Memory

In 1845, THE NOTED AMERICAN ARTIST George Peter Alexander Healy sought the next challenge in his artistic career and eventually found it in Webster's second reply to Hayne. Healy had become a much-sought-after portraitist, earning commissions from American patrons as well as the French king Louis-Philippe. The French monarch had commissioned a portrait of Webster for his burgeoning gallery of American leaders, which inspired Healy to paint a scene from Webster's January 26, 1830, speech. By early 1846, the artist had determined to begin a mammoth painting of the great debate in the Senate chamber. Capturing the moment, however, required a tremendous effort; when finished in 1851, the sixteen-by-thirty-foot tableau bore 130 individual likenesses. According to a pamphlet that advertised the painting, over 111 of the portraits had "been carefully executed by him from life."[1]

Healy approached the task with zeal, because it meant a new direction in his artistic career and a potential for greater recognition as a visual chronicler of history. In *Webster Replying to Hayne*, the artist believed he had found the perfect subject. The protagonist was a living legend adored by the northern public, especially around Boston, where Healy hoped to find a buyer for the painting. Indeed, Healy had it on good word from "certain Whigs of Boston" that someone among the city's patrons would purchase the painting and it would find a home in Faneuil Hall.[2] Bolstered by the promise of easy sale, Healy labored in his Paris studio and on trips to the United States between 1845 and 1850 to paint the individual characters from life studies. He had painted some subjects before, but others required sittings. Healy wanted to achieve historical accuracy by painting realistic portraits of the people who witnessed Webster's crowning forensic effort.

Healy's painting mixes fact with fiction in a compelling presentation of the January 26 scene. The individual portraits show many of the great leaders in astonishing detail. Webster occupies the center right of the painting, dressed in white cravat, dark blue coat with brass buttons, the dark hair combed back off his high forehead, gazing at the dais with piercing eyes. Calhoun looks back toward Webster from his perch. The audience, with the exception of an impish page modeled on the twelve-year-old son of a Senate messenger, looks intently at the Massachusetts senator. Above the boy's head looms Samuel Augustus Foot, the author of the resolution that instigated the entire affair. Hayne shows a stern gaze above the seated figure on the floor just left of center. Benton's Roman nose and cold stare give him away near the extreme right center of the painting; his wife appears almost exactly above his head in the first row of the gallery. The galleries brim with the ladies who had come to witness the effort, at odds with recollections of senators who gave their seats to women who sought to crowd the Senate floor. Another artistic license appears immediately to the left of the oval painting of Washington: John Quincy Adams looks down from the gallery, though the former president and congressman testified that he did not attend the speech. In an even more fanciful example of historical imagination, the French observer Alexis de Tocqueville appears in the top row of the gallery, a year before his arrival on American shores. Nineteen senators and fourteen representatives who served in the session appear in the portrait, though no one can confirm that all attended Webster's speech. Most, however, probably did, given the significance of the speech and the attention it received on Capitol Hill.

Completed in 1851, Healy's painting captured a defining moment in American political and constitutional history, but it met with mixed reviews from the public. "There he stands!" exclaimed one observer. "It is Daniel Webster as he appears in his moments of forensic power, sternly collected,—confident, determined; conscious of the effect of what he has said and clearly certain of what he is about to say."[3] Clearly the Godlike Daniel myth had become part of Webster lore. Art critics offered less praise. On its exhibition in New York

George Peter Alexander Healy, painter of *Webster Replying to Hayne*. Healy's tableau of the Senate on January 27, 1830, captured the mood of the momentous debate. It did not, however, meet with the financial success that its artist had hoped for. Courtesy of the Library of Congress. Reproduction number LC-USZ62-28308

on October 1851, some criticized Healy for not hewing to historical accuracy. Others questioned whether the event merited such a monumental painting. "But what shall we say about the subject itself—is it a theme for a painting?" asked the *New York Evening Post*. "A man making a speech—no matter how great the man may be, or how distinguished his auditors—is a common place affair, and no skill can elevate it into the range of Art."[4] Maybe the critic found Emanuel Leutze's *Washington Crossing the Delaware*, which had just arrived in New York, a more worthy subject for an artist's efforts.

Webster himself had viewed the painting on its first arrival in Boston in September, much to Healy's initial delight. The artist hoped that approbation from the central character would boost the painting's value and recognition. The infirm senator's reaction disappointed. Flashing a moment of humor, Webster asked Healy to identify a character in the painting. "That is Foote," replied Healy, referring to Connecticut senator Samuel Foot. "Ah, yes! Foote!

And who is that man who is looking at Foote as though he thought Foote was the great actor in the scene!" Webster responded. Finally, the sixty-nine-year-old man looked at the likeness of himself from twenty-one years earlier and dryly remarked, "I have seen handsomer men in my day."[5] The exchange had left Healy, who had hoped for an endorsement that would generate interest in the painting, somewhat disappointed.

Webster's death the following year renewed attention to the last surviving member of the Great Triumvirate. Clay had died just four months earlier, while Calhoun had left the world during the debate over the Compromise of 1850, amid another moment in which the three men betrayed fear for the future of the Union. With Webster's passing came at least some of the attention that Healy had hoped for. In December 1852, the City of Boston purchased *Webster Replying to Hayne* from its artist for $5,000, which meant that Healy took a loss on his effort. The painting found a home in Faneuil Hall, placed in a gold-gilt frame with the words "Liberty and Union Now and Forever" at its bottom, and hung above the rostrum where Webster had delivered his stirring eulogy for John Adams twenty-six years earlier.

Healy's painting recorded the moment with a stunning visual of Webster and Hayne on that January day, but the speech would receive greater fame through the generations of northern school children who memorized Webster's peroration. In many ways, remembering Webster through his words seems more fitting. His contemporaries predicted as much. The "noblest monument must be found in his works," stated Edward Everett in his eulogy to Webster. "There he will live and speak to us and our children, when brass and marble have crumbled to dust."[6] Other eulogists echoed the same sentiments. Webster's words, especially the "Second Reply to Hayne," would endure through the generations. Webster's ode to nationalism became increasingly important to observers after his death and as the Union again seemed imperiled. "The reply to Hayne settled in the minds of all reasonable men the question of State Rights and Nullification, then broached in Congress, to the great danger of the Union," argued one eulogist. "May the heavens be rolled away as a scroll, and the elements melt with fervent heat, before such sentiments shall fail of the knowledge and respect of the American people."[7]

Webster's speech became a classic exposition of nationalism and union at a time when Americans still sought to define the meaning of their nation. It took on additional significance after the Civil War settled the slavery issue and the nature of the Union at the cost of at least 620,000 lives. Americans of 1830 had feared for the future of their country; thirty years later, a civil war sundered the cords that bound it together. Thereafter, Webster's speech became a set piece on nationalism that legitimized the changed nature of nationhood in the postbellum era. Nathan Sargent, an early leader in the Republican Party and the author of an 1870s book on prominent American politicians, lauded the Webster speech as a vindication of nationalism. "That speech did more than make the name of Webster immortal," said Maryland senator Reverdy Johnson, as quoted by Sargent. "It achieved more, much more, than a triumph over the Southerner and his heresies. It fired the patriotic heart of the country. It made it rejoice that the country was ours, then and forever."[8]

Writing in 1892, historian James Ford Rhodes recounted the debate in his massive history of the United States since 1850. Rhodes portrayed the debate as high drama, with Webster seizing the moment to defend nationalism with a performance reminiscent of "the oration of Demosthenes on the Crown."[9] Rhodes noted not only the speech's significance in the history of American oratory but its lasting impact on the definition of American nationalism. "The principles he laid down are public truths," Rhodes declaimed. "It took a long war to establish them; but now, sealed in blood, they are questioned by none save Southerners of the past generation."[10]

In the hands of northern nationalists, Robert Hayne became the heretic who made the way for Webster's stirring defense of liberty and union. Rhodes argued that history would have forgotten Hayne's efforts but for the fact that they gave Webster the opportunity to respond with his brilliant remarks. Hermann von Holst, in his constitutional history of the United States, largely concurred with Rhodes, stating that the North "joyfully proclaimed Webster as the victor" while the "tone of scant assurance with which the south claimed the palm for its champion showed that it acknowledged to itself the superiority of Webster in dialectical vigor, in cutting repartee, and in the command of language."[11]

Webster's performance became the stuff of high school and college forensics, as generations of northern school children memorized his peroration. Rhodes notes in his history of the United States, written in the 1890s, that the speech had become part of the high school and college curriculum as a piece of oratory. The practice continued well into the twentieth century, with the speech appearing in textbooks and in forensics contests. A recent historian of the early American republic recalls that he memorized the peroration while in high school during the 1950s.[12] In sum, Webster's second reply to Hayne became part of the American language of nationalism and nationhood.

In twenty-first-century America, students may no longer memorize Webster's words, but the words themselves—and those of Hayne—hold critical importance to our political culture. As much as nineteenth-century observers wanted to believe that Webster had settled the issue of nationalism and states' rights, liberty and union, modern political discourse tells us otherwise. Politicians and political observers, from congressmen to ordinary people, still debate over politics within the parameters of nationalism and—or versus— states' rights. The inherent tension within our political and constitutional system between the two still shapes the way in which Americans view the role of government in their society. Informed by the past, influenced by the words of people like Webster, Hayne, and their contemporaries, encumbered by the contested legacy of American nationhood, we continue to define and redefine nationalism and states' rights in our day.

NOTES

PROLOGUE: We the States or We the People?

1. *Register of Debates*, 21st Cong., 1st Sess., 34.
2. Daniel Webster to Warren Dutton, March 8, 1830, in Edward Everett, ed., *The Writings and Speeches of Daniel Webster*, 18 vols. (New York: Little, Brown, 1903), 17:493.
3. *New York Mirror*, October 1, 1831, quoted in Robert V. Remini, *Daniel Webster: The Man and His Time* (New York: W. W. Norton, 1997), 318.

CHAPTER ONE: New England's March toward Nationalism

1. Charles M. Wiltse et al., eds., *The Papers of Daniel Webster: Public Speeches* (Dartmouth, NH: University Press of New England, 1974–1989), 1:25, 30.
2. Wiltse et al., *Papers of Daniel Webster*, 1:30; Homer Carey Hockett, *The Constitutional History of the United States, 1776–1828: The Blessings of Liberty* (New York: Macmillan, 1939), 337n25.
3. See James M. Banner Jr., *To the Hartford Convention: The Federalists and the Origins of Party Politics in Massachusetts, 1789–1815* (New York: Alfred A. Knopf, 1970), 294–350.
4. Frances Trollope, *Domestic Manners of the Americans* (London: Whittaker, Treacher, 1832).
5. *Annals of Congress*, 11th Cong., 3rd Sess., 213.
6. Ralph Ketcham, *James Madison: A Biography* (New York: Macmillan, 1971), 587.
7. James D. Richardson, ed., *Messages and Papers of the Presidents*, 10 vols. (Washington, DC: Bureau of National Research, 1897–1902), 1:562–569.
8. Richardson, *Messages and Papers*, 1:567.
9. *Annals of Congress*, 14th Cong., 1st Sess., 844.
10. *Annals of Congress*, 18th Cong., 1st Sess., 559, 565.
11. *Boston Palladium*, November 10, 1815, quoted in Shaw Livermore Jr., *The Twilight of Federalism: The Disintegration of the Federalist Party* (Princeton, NJ: Princeton University Press, 1962), 15.
12. Thomas Jefferson to Benjamin Austin, January 9, 1816, in J. Jefferson Looney, ed., *The Papers of Thomas Jefferson, Retirement Series, September 1815 to April 1816*, 13 vols. to date (Princeton, NJ: Princeton University Press, 2005–2017), 9:337.

13. See Daniel Feller, *The Jacksonian Promise: America, 1815–1840* (Baltimore: Johns Hopkins University Press, 1995), 26–30.

14. Daniel Walker Howe, *What Hath God Wrought: The Transformation of America, 1815–1848* (New York: Oxford University Press, 2007), 252.

15. Richardson, *Messages and Papers*, 2:296–297.

16. Henry Clay to Francis Preston Blair, January 29, 1825, in James F. Hopkins et al., eds., *The Papers of Henry Clay*, 11 vols. (Lexington: University Press of Kentucky, 1959–1992), 4:9–10.

17. Quoted in Samuel Flagg Bemis, *John Quincy Adams and the Union* (New York: Alfred A. Knopf, 1956), 67.

18. Bemis, *John Quincy Adams*, 76.

19. Howe, *What Hath God Wrought*, 254.

20. William Plumer to William Plumer Jr., April 24, 1820, in Everett Sommerville Brown, ed., *The Missouri Compromises and Presidential Politics, 1820–1825* (St. Louis: Missouri Historical Society, 1926), 51.

21. *Niles' Weekly Register*, November 15, 1823.

22. Howe, *What Hath God Wrought*, 142–147.

23. See Murray N. Rothbard, *The Panic of 1819: Reactions and Policies* (New York: Columbia University Press, 1962).

24. See Andrew Burstein, *The Passions of Andrew Jackson* (New York: Alfred A. Knopf, 2003), 144–145.

25. *Argus of Western America*, July 5, 1821, quoted in Amos Kendall, *Autobiography of Amos Kendall* (Boston: Lee and Shepard, 1872), 246.

26. For a superb discussion of antebellum monetary policy, see Harry L. Watson, *Liberty and Power: The Politics of Jacksonian America* (New York: Hill and Wang, 1990), 35–38.

27. For an explanation of the monetary system in the early republic, see Sharon Ann Murphy, *Other People's Money: How Banking Worked in the Early American Republic* (Baltimore: Johns Hopkins University Press, 2017), esp. 38–99.

28. William M. Gouge, *A Short History of Paper Money and Banking in the United States*, part 2 (Philadelphia: T. W. Ustick, 1833), 110.

29. See John R. Van Atta, *Securing the West: Politics, Public Lands, and the Fate of the Old Republic, 1785–1850* (Baltimore: Johns Hopkins University Press, 2014), 86–87.

30. *Annals of Congress*, 16th Cong., 1st Sess., 2036.

31. *Register of Debates*, 21st Cong., 1st Sess., 49.

CHAPTER TWO: **The South's March toward Sectionalism**

1. *Annals of Congress*, 12th Cong., 1st Sess., 442.

2. Margaret L. Coit, *John C. Calhoun: American Portrait* (New York: Houghton Mifflin, 1950), 75.

3. Quoted in Hugh A. Garland, *The Life of John Randolph of Roanoke* (New York: D. Appleton, 1853), 306.

4. Claude Bowers, *The Party Battles of the Jackson Period* (Boston: Houghton Mifflin, 1922), 89.

5. *Annals of Congress*, 12th Cong., 1st Sess., 478.

6. *Annals of Congress*, 12th Cong., 1st Sess., 480.

7. *Richmond Enquirer*, December 24, 1811.

8. Quoted in Ketcham, *James Madison*, 603.

9. Ketcham, *James Madison*, 605.

10. Charles S. Sydnor, *The Development of Southern Sectionalism, 1819–1848* (Baton Rouge: Louisiana State University Press, 1948), 105.

11. Rothbard, *The Panic of 1819*, 11–12.

12. Thomas Jefferson to John Holmes, April 22, 1820, in Merrill Peterson, ed., *Thomas Jefferson: Writings* (New York: Library of America, 1984), 1433.

13. *Annals of Congress*, 15th Cong., 2nd Sess., 1170.

14. For a brief summary of the case and its implications, see Feller, *The Jacksonian Promise*, 48–50.

15. *Richmond Enquirer*, March 30, 1819.

16. *Richmond Enquirer*, June 11, 1819.

17. *Richmond Enquirer*, July 23, 1819.

18. Quoted in Coit, *Calhoun*, 147.

19. Noble E. Cunningham Jr., *The Presidency of James Monroe* (Lawrence: University Press of Kansas, 1996), 103–104.

20. Sean Wilentz, *The Politicians and the Egalitarians: The Hidden History of American Politics* (New York: W. W. Norton, 2016), 34–35.

21. George McDuffie, *Defence of a Liberal Construction of the Powers of Congress, as Regards Internal Improvement, Etc.* (Philadelphia: William F. Geddes, 1832), 20.

22. George McDuffie, *Defence of a Liberal Construction of the Powers of Congress, as Regards Internal Improvement, Etc.* (Philadelphia: William F. Geddes, 1832), 19.

23. George McDuffie, *National and State Rights, Considered by the Hon. George M'Duffie, Under the Signature of "One of the People"* . . . (Columbia, SC: Free Press and Hive Office, 1831), 19–20.

24. See John Lauritz Larson, *Internal Improvement: National Public Works and the Promise of Popular Government in the Early United States* (Chapel Hill: University of North Carolina Press, 2001), 146.

25. *Annals of Congress*, 16th Cong., 1st Sess., 2032.

26. *Annals of Congress*, 18th Cong., 2nd Sess., 649.

27. *Register of Debates*, 19th Cong., 2nd Sess., 329.

28. Quoted in William W. Freehling, *The Road to Disunion*, vol. 1, *Secessionists at Bay, 1776–1854* (New York: Oxford University Press, 1990), 257.

29. My description of South Carolina is derived from Freehling, *Road to Disunion*, 1:254–257.

30. Martin Van Buren to Thomas A. Ritchie, January 13, 1827, Martin Van Buren Papers, Library of Congress.

31. Josiah Stoddard Johnston to Henry Clay, May 9, 1828, in Hopkins et al., *The Papers of Henry Clay*, 7:263–264.

32. For the view that Van Buren intentionally created a tariff schedule that northeasterners would reject, see Feller, *Jacksonian Promise*, 72–73. For the argument that Van Buren helped write the bill in earnest hope that it would pass, see John Niven, *Martin Van Buren: The Romantic Age of American Politics* (New York: Oxford University Press, 1983), 197–199.

33. See John Niven, *John C. Calhoun and the Price of Union: A Biography* (Baton Rouge: Louisiana State University Press, 1988), 130–134.

34. "Address on the Relation with the States and the General Government Bear to Each Other [July 26, 1831], in Richard K. Cralle, ed., *Reports and Public Letters of John C. Calhoun* (New York: D. Appleton, 1870), 69.

35. Freehling, Road to Disunion, 1:257.

36. Dangerfield, *Awakening of American Nationalism*, 284.

37. "Exposition," in Cralle, *Reports and Public Letters of John C. Calhoun*, 25–26. This is the original draft of the document. The South Carolina legislature heavily amended the document before its adoption. See Charles M. Wiltse, *John C. Calhoun: Nationalist, 1782–1828* (Indianapolis: Bobbs-Merrill, 1944), 393.

CHAPTER THREE: **The West Asserts Its Power**

1. *Register of Debates*, 21st Cong., 1st Sess., 3.

2. *Register of Debates*, 21st Cong., 1st Sess., 4.

3. *Register of Debates*, 21st Cong., 1st Sess., 4–5.

4. *Register of Debates*, 21st Cong., 1st Sess., 477. See Van Atta, *Securing the West*, 139–140.

5. Merrill D. Peterson, *The Great Triumvirate: Webster, Clay, and Calhoun* (New York: Oxford University Press, 1987), 170. For examples of the traditional interpretation of Foot's resolution as an innocuous measure, see Peterson, *The Great Triumvirate*; Peter C. Hoffer, "Sectionalism and National History: American History in the Debate over Foote's Resolution, December 1829–May 1830," *Missouri Historical Review* 66 (1972): 520–538. More recently, John Van Atta has taken issue with this interpretation; see his *Securing the West*, 142–145.

6. For Benton, see William Nisbet Chambers, *Old Bullion Benton, Senator from the New West: Thomas Hart Benton, 1782–1858* (Boston: Little, Brown, 1956); Elbert B. Smith, *Magnificent Missourian: The Life of Thomas Hart Benton* (Philadelphia: J. B. Lippincott, 1957).

7. Thomas Hart Benton, *Thirty Years' View; or a History of the Working of the American Government for Thirty Years, from 1820 to 1850*, 2 vols. (New York: D. Appleton, 1854), 1:5.

8. See Daniel Feller, *The Public Lands in Jacksonian Politics* (Madison: University of Wisconsin Press, 1984), 26–35; Van Atta, *Securing the West*, 85–87.

9. Van Atta, *Securing the West*, 86–87.

10. *Register of Debates*, 19th Cong., 1st Sess., 727.

11. Larson, *Internal Improvement*, 141–148.

12. *Annals of Congress*, 18th Cong., 1st Sess., 1038; Feller, *The Public Lands in Jacksonian Politics*, 60.

13. *Annals of Congress*, 18th Cong., 1st Sess., 1298–1299.

14. *Annals of Congress*, 18th Cong., 1st Sess., 1316–1317.

15. Larson, *Internal Improvement*, 145–148.

16. *Register of Debates*, 19th Cong., 1st Sess., 358–359.

17. *Register of Debates*, 19th Cong., 1st Sess., 762.

18. *Register of Debates*, 19th Cong., 1st Sess., 762. See also Feller, *The Public Lands in Jacksonian Politics*, 74–75.

19. Chambers, *Old Bullion Benton*, 133–135.

20. *Register of Debates*, 19th Cong., 1st Sess., 727. For Benton's speech, see pp. 720–749.

21. *Register of Debates*, 19th Cong., 1st Sess., 725.

22. *Register of Debates*, 19th Cong., 1st Sess., 729.

23. Quoted in Feller, *The Public Lands in Jacksonian Politics*, 76.

24. Charles Francis Adams, ed., *Memoirs of John Quincy Adams*, 12 vols. (Philadelphia: J. B. Lippincott, 1874–1877), 7:188, 194.

25. *Annals of Congress*, 18th Cong., 1st Sess., 1972.

26. See Van Atta, *Securing the West*, 129–130.

27. Richardson, *Messages and Papers*, 2:391.

28. *Register of Debates*, 20th Cong., 1st Sess., 2831–2832.

29. See Chambers, *Old Bullion Benton*, 135–136; Feller, *The Public Lands in Jacksonian Politics*, 92–95.

30. *Register of Debates*, 20th Cong., 1st Sess., 15–16.

31. *Register of Debates*, 20th Cong., 1st Sess., 151.

32. *Register of Debates*, 20th Cong., 1st Sess., 508.

33. *Register of Debates*, 20th Cong., 1st Sess., 656; Feller, *The Public Lands in Jacksonian Politics*, 95.

34. For the graduation vote, see *Register of Debates*, 20th Cong., 1st Sess., 678.

35. Quoted in Feller, *The Public Lands in Jacksonian Politics*, 103.

36. For the election of 1828, see Lynn Hudson Parsons, *The Birth of Modern Politics: Andrew Jackson, John Quincy Adams, and the Election of 1828* (New York: Oxford University Press, 2009); Donald B. Cole, *Vindicating Andrew Jackson: The 1828 Election and the Rise of the Two-Party System* (Lawrence: University Press of Kansas, 2009).

37. Daniel Webster to Samuel Bell, July 29, 1828, in Wiltse et al., *Papers of Daniel Webster: Correspondence*, 2:356.

38. *American State Papers: Public Lands*, 5:582–583, 622–623.

39. *American State Papers: Public Lands*, 5:622.

40. Quoted in Van Atta, *Securing the West*, 137.

41. Duff Green to Ninian Edwards, December 22, 1828, and January 6, 1829, in E. B. Washburne, ed., *The Edwards Papers* (Chicago: Fergus, 1884), 379, 380.

42. *American State Papers: Public Lands*, 5:630.

43. See *American State Papers: Public Lands*, vol. 5, especially the memorials from the 20th Congress, for examples.

44. *Register of Debates*, 20th Cong., 1st Sess., 505–507, 577–582; Edward Everett, "The Debate in the Senate of the United States," *North American Review* 31 (October 1830): 467–469.

45. *American State Papers: Public Lands*, 5:793.

46. *American State Papers: Public Lands*, 5:796.

47. Richardson, *Messages and Papers*, 2:882.

CHAPTER FOUR: **The Great Debate**

1. *Register of Debates*, 21st Cong., 1st Sess., 80.

2. Quoted in George Ticknor Curtis, *Life of Daniel Webster*, 2 vols. (New York: D. Appleton, 1893), 1:276.

3. "Adams and Jefferson," August 2, 1826, in Wiltse, et al., *Papers of Daniel Webster: Speeches and Formal Writings*, 1:255–256.

4. Daniel Webster to Jeremiah Mason, February 27, 1830, in Wiltse et al., *Papers of Daniel Webster: Correspondence*, 3:19.

5. Feller, *The Public Lands in Jacksonian Politics*, 68–69; Van Atta, *Securing the West*, 102–103; *American State Papers: Public Lands*, 5:624–625. For Edwards's role in the cession proposal, see Van Atta, *Securing the West*, 134–138; Feller, *The Public Lands in Jacksonian Politics*, 107–109.

6. Feller, *The Public Lands in Jacksonian Politics*, 111.

7. *Register of Debates*, 21st Cong., 1st Sess., 4, 6.

8. *Register of Debates*, 21st Cong., 1st Sess., 23, 22, 23.

9. Benton, *Thirty Years' View*, 1:130, 131. For the range of northeastern opinion on the land issue, see Van Atta, *Securing the West*, 146–147.

10. Chambers, *Old Bullion Benton*, 139; Larson, *Internal Improvements*, 164.

11. See Van Atta, *Securing the West*, 146–147.

12. *Register of Debates*, 21st Cong., 1st Sess., 24.

13. On Hayne, see Theodore D. Jervey, *Robert Y. Hayne and His Times* (New York: Macmillan, 1909); Freehling, *Prelude to Civil War*, 103–104.

14. Quoted in Jervey, *Robert Y. Hayne*, 223.

15. For a thorough discussion of the different strains of states' rights ideology prior to the nullification crisis, see Richard E. Ellis, *The Union at Risk: Jacksonian Democracy, States' Rights, and the Nullification Crisis* (New York: Oxford University Press, 1987), 5–9.

16. Freehling, *Prelude to Civil War*, 89–133; Forrest McDonald, *States' Rights and the Union: Imperium in Imperio, 1776–1876* (Lawrence: University Press of Kansas, 2000), 103–106.

17. Ellis, *The Union at Risk*, 7–9.

18. For Hayne's first speech, see *Register of Debates*, 21st Cong., 1st Sess., 31–35.

19. *Register of Debates,* 21st Cong., 1st Sess., 32.

20. *Register of Debates,* 21st Cong., 1st Sess., 32.

21. *Register of Debates,* 21st Cong., 1st Sess., 32.

22. *Register of Debates,* 21st Cong., 1st Sess., 33.

23. *Register of Debates,* 21st Cong., 1st Sess., 32, 33, 34.

24. *Register of Debates,* 21st Cong., 1st Sess., 34.

25. *Register of Debates,* 21st Cong., 1st Sess., 34.

26. Feller, *The Public Lands in Jacksonian Politics,* 119–125.

27. See Feller, *The Public Lands in Jacksonian Politics,* 119–136.

28. For Webster's account of how he became involved in the debate, see Daniel Webster to Jeremiah Mason, February 27, 1830, in Wiltse et al., *Papers of Daniel Webster: Correspondence,* 3:18–20.

29. *Niles' National Register,* March 23, 1844, 55.

30. For Webster's views on graduation, see Van Atta, *Securing the West,* 160–163.

31. For Webster's action on the South Carolina railroad, see *Register of Debates,* 21st Cong., 1st Sess., 21–22; Peterson, *The Great Triumvirate,* 172.

32. Harlow W. Sheidley, "The Webster-Hayne Debate: Recasting New England's Sectionalism," *New England Quarterly* 67 (March 1994): 5–29, quote on 9.

33. Peter J. Parish, "Daniel Webster, New England, and the West," *Journal of American History* 54 (December 1967): 524–549; Remini, *Daniel Webster,* 317–318. For Webster's use of the lands question, see Van Atta, *Securing the West,* 162–163.

34. For Webster's first reply to Hayne, see *Register of Debates,* 21st Cong., 1st Sess., 35–41.

35. *Register of Debates,* 21st Cong., 1st Sess., 36. See Peter S. Onuf, *Statehood and Union: A History of the Northwest Ordinance* (Bloomington: Indiana University Press, 1987), 141–145. For Webster's efforts to rehabilitate New England's reputation, see Sheidley, "The Webster-Hayne Debate."

36. See Feller, *The Public Lands in Jacksonian Politics,* 124.

37. *Register of Debates,* 21st Cong., 1st Sess., 40.

38. *Register of Debates,* 21st Cong., 1st Sess., 38. For the original speech by Thomas Cooper, see *Niles' Weekly Register,* September 8, 1827, 28–32.

39. *Register of Debates,* 21st Cong., 1st Sess., 38–39.

40. Maurice G. Baxter, *One and Inseparable: Daniel Webster and the Union* (Cambridge, MA: Harvard University Press, 1984), 183.

41. For Hayne's second speech, see *Register of Debates,* Senate, 21st Cong., 1st Sess., 43–58.

42. Historians still dispute whether Calhoun passed notes to Hayne. Webster biographer Robert Remini tends to support the story; others omit the story.

43. See *Register of Debates,* 21st Cong., 1st Sess., 43–58, for Hayne's speech.

44. *Register of Debates,* 21st Cong., 1st Sess., 48.

45. Quoted in Remini, *Daniel Webster,* 324.

46. Peter Harvey, *Reminiscences and Anecdotes of Daniel Webster* (Boston: Little, Brown, 1878), 156.

47. Quoted in Charles W. March, *Daniel Webster and His Contemporaries*, 4th ed. (New York: Mason, Baker & Pratt, 1873), 124–125.

48. Harvey, *Reminiscences*, 150.

49. Remini, *Daniel Webster*, 324.

50. For the original text of Webster's second reply to Hayne, see *Register of Debates*, 21st Cong., 1st Sess., 58–80. Webster revised Gales's transcription for publication. In this text, I follow the revised version; see Wiltse et al., *Papers of Daniel Webster: Speeches and Formal Writings*, 1:349–393.

51. [Henry W. Hilliard], "Daniel Webster and the Constitution," *Harper's Magazine* 54 (1876): 599–600.

52. *Register of Debates*, 21st Cong., 1st Sess., 77.

53. Quoted in Harvey, *Reminiscences*, 153.

CHAPTER FIVE: **Nullification and Nationhood**

1. Quoted in James Parton, *Life of Andrew Jackson*, 3 vols. (Boston: Houghton Mifflin, 1859–1860), 3:282.

2. Richardson, *Messages and Papers*,2:1015.

3. Richardson, *Messages and Papers*, 2:1010–1011.

4. See Jon Meacham, *American Lion: Andrew Jackson in the White House* (New York: Random House, 2008), 130; Robert V. Remini, *Andrew Jackson and the Course of American Freedom, 1822–1832* (New York: Harper and Row, 1981), 232–233; William B. Hatcher, *Edward Livingston: Jeffersonian Republican and Jacksonian Democrat* (Baton Rouge: Louisiana State University Press, 1940), 348–349.

5. Peterson, *The Great Triumvirate*, 179.

6. See Sheidley, "The Webster-Hayne Debate."

7. Feller, *The Jacksonian Promise*, 163.

8. *Register of Debates*, 21st Cong., 1st Sess., 111.

9. *Register of Debates*, 21st Cong., 1st Sess., 133.

10. *Register of Debates*, 21st Cong., 1st Sess., 137.

11. *Register of Debates*, 21st Cong., 1st Sess., 141.

12. *Register of Debates*, 21st Cong., 1st Sess., 227.

13. *Register of Debates*, 21st Cong., 1st Sess., 228.

14. *Register of Debates*, 21st Cong., 1st Sess., 229.

15. *Register of Debates*, 21st Cong., 1st Sess., 229.

16. Hatcher, *Edward Livingston*, 348. For Livingston's speech, see *Register of Debates*, 21st Cong., 1st Sess., 247–272.

17. *Register of Debates*, 21st Cong., 1st Sess., 247–272. See also Ellis, *The Union at Risk*, 11–12; Hatcher, *Edward Livingston*, 345–351. For Livingston's remarks on internal improvements, see Hatcher, *Edward Livingston*, 304–305; *Annals of Congress*, 18th Cong., 1st Sess., 1429–1459.

18. *Register of Debates*, 21st Cong., 1st Sess., 255, 272.

19. James Madison to Edward Livingston, May 8, 1830, *Founders Online*, Na-

tional Archives, last modified July 12, 2016, http://founders.archives.gov/documents/Madison/99-02-02-2038.

20. "[Copy of James Madison] to Robert Y. Hayne [as enclosed in James Madison to Edward Everett, April 17, 1830], 3 April 1830," *Founders Online*, National Archives, last modified July 12, 2016, http://founders.archives.gov/documents/Madison/99-02-02-2017. See also Irving Brant, *James Madison: Commander in Chief, 1812–1836* (Indianapolis: Bobbs-Merrill, 1961), 479–480.

21. Martin Van Buren, *The Autobiography of Martin Van Buren*, in John C. Fitzpatrick, ed., *Annual Report of the American Historical Association for the Year 1918* (Washington, DC: Government Printing Office, 1918), 412.

22. Van Buren, *Autobiography*, 414.

23. Quoted in Remini, *Andrew Jackson and the Course of American Freedom*, 235.

24. Quoted in Remini, *Andrew Jackson and the Course of American Freedom*, 235. See also Van Buren, *Autobiography*, 416.

25. Van Buren, *Autobiography*, 415.

26. Van Buren, *Autobiography*, 415.

27. Van Buren, *Autobiography*, 415.

28. Van Buren, *Autobiography*, 415.

29. For full accounts of the dinner, see Van Buren, *Autobiography*, 413–417; Remini, *Andrew Jackson and the Course of American Freedom*, 233–236.

30. Amos Kendall to Francis P. Blair, April 25, 1830, in Robert V. Remini, ed., *The Age of Jackson* (New York: Harper and Row, 1972), 151.

31. Parton, *Life of Jackson*, 3:284–285.

32. Quoted in Remini, *Andrew Jackson and the Course of American Freedom*, 70.

33. Richardson, *Messages and Papers*, 2:1153.

34. David F. Ericson, "The Nullification Crisis, American Republicanism, and the Force Bill Debate," *Journal of Southern History* 61 (May 1995): 249–270.

35. Quoted in Niven, *Calhoun and the Price of Union*, 182.

36. Quoted in Feller, *Jacksonian Promise*, 165.

37. *Columbia Telescope Extra*, December 13, 1832.

38. Quoted in Freehling, *Prelude to Civil War*, 265.

39. Drew R. McCoy, *The Last of the Fathers: James Madison and the Republican Legacy* (New York: Cambridge University Press, 1989), 147–148; Meacham, *American Lion*, 227.

40. Richardson, *Messages and Papers*, 4:1211.

41. Richardson, *Messages and Papers*, 4:1211.

42. Robert V. Remini, *Andrew Jackson and the Course of American Democracy, 1833–1845* (New York: Harper & Row, 1984), 21.

43. Richardson, *Messages and Papers*, 4:1217.

44. For Webster's speech, see *Register of Debates*, 22nd Cong., 2nd Sess., 409–413.

45. For Calhoun's speech, see *Register of Debates*, 22nd Cong., 2nd Sess., 519–553.

46. For Webster's speech, see *Register of Debates*, 22nd Cong., 2nd Sess., 554–587.

47. *Register of Debates*, 22nd Cong., 2nd Sess., 554–587.

48. *Register of Debates*, Senate, 22nd Cong., 2nd Sess., 554–587.
49. March, *Daniel Webster and His Contemporaries*, 242–243.
50. Andrew Jackson to Joel Poinsett, February 17, 1833, quoted in Remini, *Daniel Webster*, 380.
51. Peterson, *The Great Triumvirate*, 219.
52. Daniel Webster to Joseph Hopkinson, February 9, 1833, in Wiltse et al., *Papers of Daniel Webster: Correspondence*, 3:213.
53. See Ellis, *The Union at Risk*, 165–170.
54. Peterson, *The Great Triumvirate*, 232.
55. *Register of Debates*, 21st Cong., 1st Sess., 49.
56. Remini, *Andrew Jackson and the Course of American Freedom*, 235. For the significance of the election of 1828 and the context of the so-called second party system, see Donald B. Cole, *Vindicating Andrew Jackson: The 1828 Election and the Rise of the Two-Party System* (Lawrence: University Press of Kansas, 2009); Lynn Hudson Parsons, *The Birth of Modern Politics: Andrew Jackson, John Quincy Adams, and the Election of 1828* (New York: Oxford University Press, 2009).

EPILOGUE: The Webster-Hayne Debate in Historical Memory

1. Quoted in Frederick Voss, "Webster Replying to Hayne: George Healy and the Economics of History Painting," *American Art* 15 (Fall 2001): 40.
2. Voss, "Webster Replying to Hayne," 38.
3. *Boston Transcript*, December 18, 1852, quoted in Remini, *Daniel Webster*, 709.
4. *New York Evening Post*, October 1, 1851, quoted in Voss, "Webster Replying to Hayne," 48.
5. *New York Evening Post*, September 27, 1851, quoted in Voss, "Webster Replying to Hayne," 48.
6. Edward Everett, "Eulogy in Boston," quoted in Charles Lanman, *The Private Life of Daniel Webster* (New York: Harper and Brothers, 1852), 196.
7. Wilbur M. Haywood, "Eulogy," in *The Life, Eulogy, and Orations of Daniel Webster* (Rochester: Wilbur M. Haywood, 1853), 61.
8. Quoted in Nathan Sargent, *Public Men and Events from the Commencement of Mr. Monroe's Administration, in 1817, to the Close of Mr. Fillmore's Administration, in 1853*, 2 vols. (Philadelphia: J. B. Lippincott, 1875), 1:173.
9. James Ford Rhodes, *History of the United States from the Compromise of 1850*, 8 vols., (New York: Macmillan, 1892–1906), 1:43.
10. Rhodes, *History of the United States*, 1:43.
11. Hermann von Holst, *The Constitutional and Political History of the United States*, 8 vols. (Chicago: Callaghan, 1877–1892), 1:470.
12. Howe, *What Hath God Wrought*, 371.

SUGGESTED FURTHER READING

This essay provides a collection of sources that pertain to the Webster-Hayne Debate and its significance to the Union, though for reasons of brevity it does not offer a comprehensive collection of all the literature on nationalism and sectionalism in the early American republic. Consulting the bibliographies of the works cited here will provide an even broader collection for students of the era.

For the Webster-Hayne Debate itself, the starting point is the speeches themselves, many of which are collected in Herman Belz, ed., *The Webster-Hayne Debate on the Nature of the Union* (Indianapolis, 2000). The Belz collection contains a useful introduction as well that outlines the major themes discussed during the debate. All the speeches are in the *Register of Debates*. Few other books address the debate alone. Stefan M. Brooks analyzes the debate from the perspective of a political scientist in *The Webster-Hayne Debate: An Inquiry into the Nature of the Union* (Lanham, MD, 2009). Harlow W. Sheidley investigates the debate from the New England perspective in "The Webster-Hayne Debate: Recasting New England's Sectionalism," *New England Quarterly* 67 (1995): 5–29.

The debate over nationalism and sectionalism has garnered the attention of numerous scholars. Essential works include Forrest McDonald, *States' Rights and the Union: Imperium in Imperio, 1776–1876* (Lawrence, KS, 2000); Jesse T. Carpenter, *The South as a Conscious Minority* (New York, 1930); Major L. Wilson, *Space, Time, and Freedom: The Quest for Nationality and the Irrepressible Conflict,1815–1861* (Westport, CT, 1974). Elizabeth Varon's *Disunion! The Coming of the American Civil War, 1789–1859* (Chapel Hill, 2008) provides important context in terms of the permanency of the Union.

One of the major protagonists has attracted many able biographers; the other has but one. The best and most thorough recent biography of Daniel Webster is Robert V. Remini, *Daniel Webster: The Man and His Time* (New York, 1997). Two other recent biographies merit attention: Irving Bartlett, *Daniel Webster* (New York, 1978); Maurice G. Baxter, *One and Inseparable: Daniel Webster and the Union* (Cambridge, MA, 1984). Robert Y. Hayne's only biographer, Theodore D. Jervey, wrote more than one hundred years ago; the book, *Robert Y. Hayne and His Times* (New York, 1909), is badly outdated but remains the major source. Other biographies that study the people involved in the debate illuminate key issues. Merrill Peterson's *The Great Triumvirate: Webster, Clay, and Calhoun* (New York, 1987) offers a masterful group portrait of three of the most influential American politicians of the time. Clay receives thorough treatment in Robert V. Remini, *Henry Clay: Statesman for the Union* (New York, 1991) and David S. Heidler and Jeanne T. Heidler, *Henry Clay: The Essential American* (New York, 2010). The best brief biography of Calhoun is John Niven, *John C. Calhoun and the Price of Union* (Baton Rouge, 1988). For a more comprehensive treatment, see the classic three-volume biography by Charles M. Wiltse, *John C. Calhoun* (Indianapolis, 1944–1951). Two biographers in the 1950s chronicled the life of Thomas Hart Benton; neither effort proves entirely satisfying. William Nisbet Chambers, *Old Bullion Benton, Senator from the New West: Thomas Hart Benton, 1782–1858* (Boston, 1956) is the better of the two; see also Elbert Smith, *Magnificent Missourian: The Life of Thomas Hart Benton* (Philadelphia, 1957). Edward Livingston's efforts to see a common ground between Webster and Hayne's positions on the nature of the Union gain mention in William B. Hatcher, *Edward Livingston: Jeffersonian Republican and Jacksonian Democrat* (Baton Rouge, 1940).

Presidential biographies also provide insight into the debates. John Quincy Adams has received much attention in recent years, but the best treatment is William J. Cooper, *The Lost Founding Father: John Quincy Adams and the Transformation of American Politics* (New York, 2017). See also James Traub, *John Quincy Adams: Militant Spirit* (New York, 2016) and the classic Samuel Flagg Bemis, *John Quincy Adams and the Union* (New York, 1956). Andrew Jackson has attracted a legion of biographers; see Jon Meacham's artfully written *American Lion: Andrew Jackson in the White House* (New York, 2008) and Robert V. Remini's encyclopedic three-volume *Andrew Jackson* (New York, 1977–1984). Former President James Madison played an important secondary role in the debate, which receives attention in Ralph Ketcham, *James Madison* (New York, 1971) and Drew McCoy's brilliant *The Last of the Fathers: James Madison and the Republican Legacy* (Cambridge, MA, 1989).

Histories of the United States after the War of 1812 provide the context necessary to understand the origins of the debate. Daniel Walker Howe's *What Hath God Wrought: The Transformation of America, 1815–1848* (New York, 2007) provides the most recent and most comprehensive history of the period. Harry L. Watson's *Liberty and Power: The Politics of Jacksonian America* (New York, 1990) offers a solid interpretive framework for the Jacksonian era. Students should also consult Daniel Feller, *The Jacksonian Promise: America, 1815–1840* (Baltimore, 1995), a superb treatment of the period. Historians have largely neglected the so-called Era of Good Feelings. Though dated, George Dangerfield's *The Awakening of American Nationalism, 1815–1828* (New York, 1965) treats all the major themes that contributed to the debate. For an older but still useful view of southerners' drift from nationalism, see Charles S. Sydnor, *The Development of Southern Sectionalism, 1819–1848* (Baton Rouge, 1948). Shaw Livermore Jr., *The Twilight of Federalism* (Princeton, 1962), analyzes the collapse of the old political party and its impact on politics in the 1820s.

Economic issues played a major role in provoking the debate. They receive treatment in the surveys cited above, but detailed studies complete the story. The Market Revolution receives thorough, if idiosyncratic, treatment in Charles Sellers's *The Market Revolution: Jacksonian America, 1815–1846* (New York, 1991). John Lauritz

Larson has written two important books on economic history during the period: *The Market Revolution in America: Liberty, Ambition, and the Eclipse of the Common Good* (Cambridge, 2010), a brief survey, and *Internal Improvement: National Public Works and the Promise of Popular Government in the Early United States* (Chapel Hill, 2001), which analyzes the debate over national economic development and public works. Murray N. Rothbard, *The Panic of 1819: Reactions and Policies* (New York, 1962) studies the depression that ended the 1810s western land bubble. Two older works remain essential for understanding the changing economic trends in the years after the War of 1812: Douglass C. North, *The Economic Growth of the United States, 1790–1860* (New York, 1961), and George Rogers Taylor, *The Transportation Revolution, 1815–1860* (New York, 1951).

On western land policy as the catalyst for the Foot resolution and the Webster-Hayne Debate itself, two works are essential. John R. Van Atta's *Securing the West: Politics, Public Lands, and the Fate of the Old Republic, 1785–1850* (Baltimore, 2014) rightfully restores the role of land policy as much more than a sideshow to the debate. Daniel Feller's *The Public Lands in Jacksonian Politics* (Madison, 1984) covers every angle of the land issue, its origins, and its significance to Jacksonian era politics. The biographies of Thomas Hart Benton supplement both works, as does Benton's own *Thirty Years' View*, 2 vols. (New York, 1854).

Two books address the peculiar circumstances in South Carolina that led to nullification. William W. Freehling, *Prelude to Civil War: The Nullification Controversy in South Carolina, 1816–1836* (New York, 1965), captures the unique politics of the Palmetto State and the paranoia among its ruling elite. It also treats the labyrinthine politics of the tariff skillfully. Richard E. Ellis, *The Union at Risk: Jacksonian Democracy, States' Rights, and the Nullification Crisis* (New York, 1987) addresses the political and constitutional issues at stake by connecting South Carolina's nullifiers to national developments.

The Webster-Hayne Debate has long received the attention of scholars for its spirited forensics and as a superb example of political oratory in the early nineteenth century. Several works study the importance of speechmaking and listening to speeches in the early American republic, not just among elites like Daniel Webster and Robert Hayne. Kenneth Cmiel, *Democratic Eloquence: The Fight over Popular Speech in Nineteenth-Century America* (New York, 1990), focuses on the democratization of oratory as a parallel to the political trends of the time. Carolyn Eastman, *A Nation of Speechifiers: Making an American Republic after the Revolution* (Chicago, 2009), illustrates how common people became versed in oratory and how it united people before American nationalism had coalesced.

INDEX

Adams, John, 40

Adams, John Quincy: Compromise of 1833, 135; death of, 86; economic policy, 18, 19, 125; and election of 1828, 79; and Missouri crisis, 43; as a nationalist, x, 12, 51; as presidential candidate (1824), 20, 21, 23, 46; supports American system, 61; in *Webster Replying to Hayne*, 141; and western politics, 71, 74, 78–79

agriculture, and southern cotton economy, 38

Alabama, 24; and nullification, 128; and Panic of 1819, 38; westward expansion, 24, 37

American System, 13, 21, 22, 117; Clay as author, 11; and Andrew Jackson, 124; opposition to, 14, 15, 49; and Panic of 1819, 30; support for, 19, 61; Webster supports, 105; and western interests, 72

Astor, John Jacob, 1, 100

banking, United States, 26–27; and land speculation, 37, 38

Bank of the United States, 13, 38; demise of first bank, 10; and *McCulloch v. Maryland*, 40; and Panic of 1819, 26; recharter, 15; regulatory power, 28; southern opposition to, 38; supported by Madison, 12; western resentment, 63

Barton, David, 67, 77

Benton, Thomas Hart, 62–63; alliance with southern senators, 75; first speech in Webster-Hayne Debate, 90–91; graduation land policy, 67–68, 69–70, 77; opposes Foot resolution, 60, 89; opposition to Webster, 103, 106, 117

Boston Manufacturing Company, 18

Burr, Aaron, 72

Calhoun, John C., 11–12; author of *Exposition and Protest*, 56–59; as economic nationalist, 11, 32, 44; and Force Bill, 132–33; Fort Hill address, 109; House of Representatives career, 13; and Jefferson Day dinner, 122–23; mentor to Hayne, ix, 93; Missouri crisis, 43; opposition to tariffs, 52, 94; on ordinance of nullification, 132; presidential candidate, 1824, 23; resigns vice-presidency, 128; response to Hayne's first speech, 109; tariff of 1828, 54–56; vice-president, 2, 128; War Hawk, 5, 34; in *Webster Replying to Hayne*, 141

Carroll, William, 26

Carver v. Jackson (1830), 100

cession, federal lands, 68, 73; failure in Congress, 77, 84

Cheves, Langdon, 92

Civil War, 143

Clay, Henry, 10; and American System, 30; and Compromise of 1833, 135–36; death of, 143; distribution policy, 73; origins of American System, 10; presidential candidate, 1824, 20, 21, 23; Speaker of the House, 13, 34; War Hawk, 5; and western land policy, 66–67

Clayton, John M., 118

Clinton, George, 10

compact theory of Union, 120; and *Exposition and Protest*, 57

Compromise of 1833, 135–36

congressional nominating caucus, 20, 22

Constitution, U.S.: federal supremacy, 133; interpretation of, 120; necessary and proper clause, 41; slavery in the territories, 43

Cooper, Thomas, 51, 52, 94; remarks on Union, 105